☼

CARVED IN STONE

☼

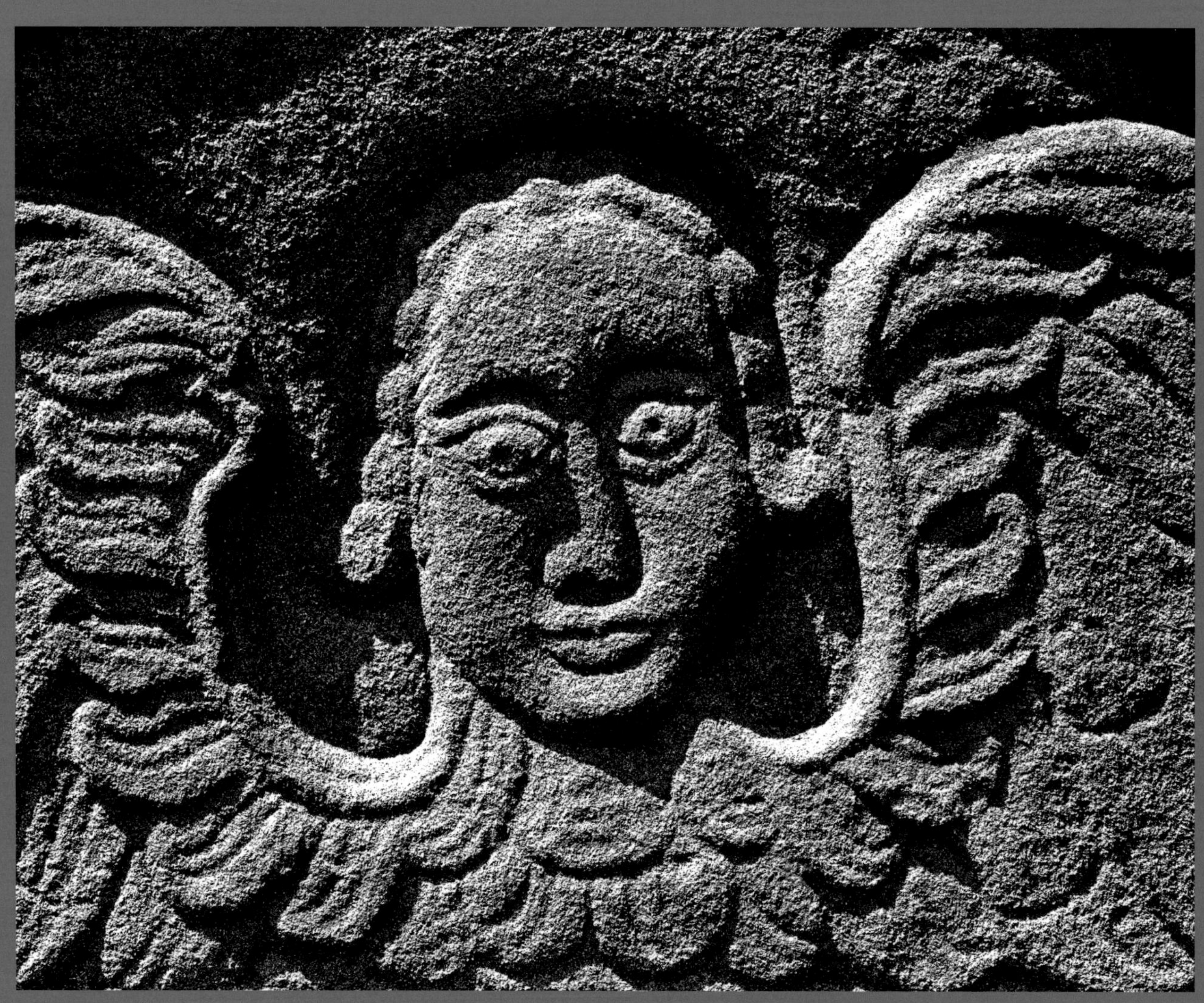

Photographs by Thomas E. Gilson ✲ *Essay by William Gilson*

CARVED IN STONE

THE ARTISTRY OF EARLY NEW ENGLAND GRAVESTONES

Wesleyan University Press ✲ *Middletown, Connecticut*

Wesleyan University Press
Middletown CT 06459
www.wesleyan.edu/wespress

Manufactured in China
First paperback edition 2024
Paperback ISBN 978-0-8195-0124-0
Designed by Mindy Basinger Hill
Typeset in Adobe Jenson Pro

The essay portion of this book was first published as "Stone Faces," along with twelve photographs, in the *New England Review.*

The Library of Congress cataloged the hardcover edition as:
Gilson, Thomas.
Carved in stone: the artistry of early New England gravestones / photographs by Thomas E. Gilson; essay by William Gilson.
p. cm.
Includes bibliographical references.
ISBN 978-0-8195-7301-8 (cloth: alk. paper)
ISBN 978-0-8195-7302-5 (ebook)
1. Cemeteries—New England—Pictorial works.
2. Sepulchral monuments—New England—Pictorial works.
3. NewEngland—History—Colonial period, ca. 1600–1775.
I. Gilson, William. II. Title.
F5.G55 2012
363.7'50974—dc23 2012010810

5 4 3 2 1

For Carolyn, Ethan, and Jimena

THOMAS E. GILSON

☼ ☼ ☼

For Alison, Tom, and Joe

WILLIAM GILSON

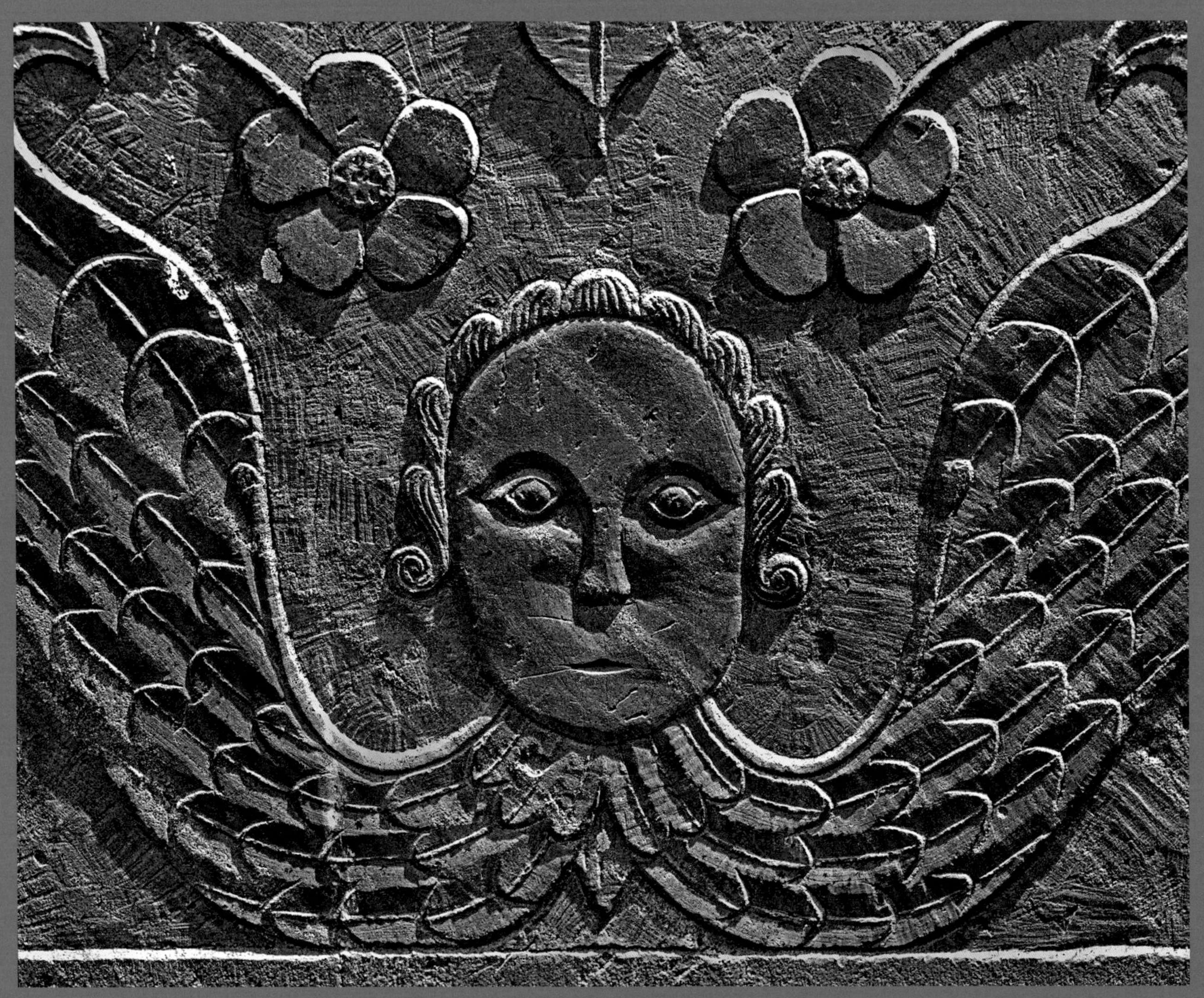

CONTENTS

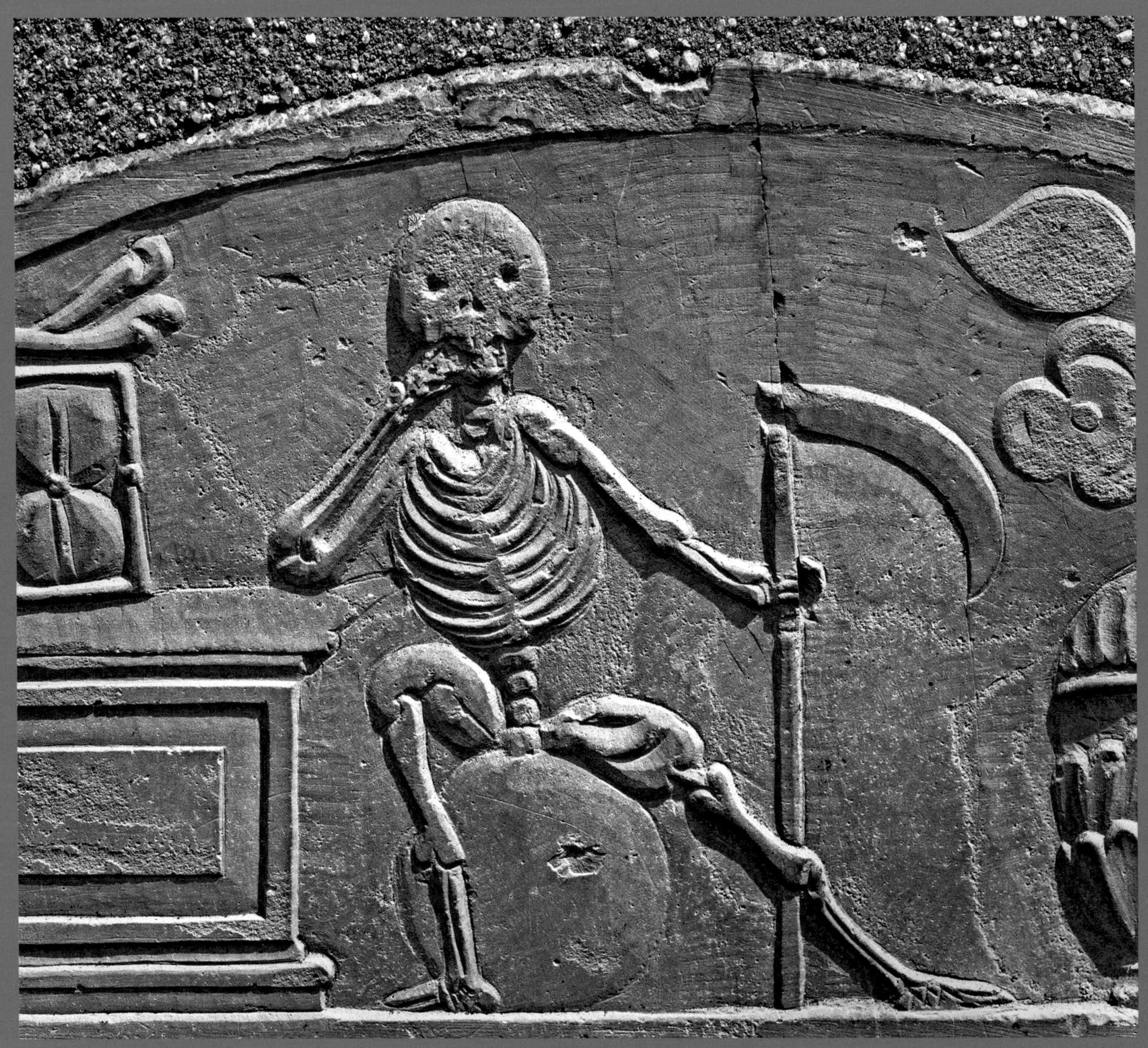

PREFACE

The early New England settlers found themselves in a harsh, unfamiliar environment, looking for a new beginning. What they brought with them were their skills, ingenuity, and, more than anything else, their perseverance and their religious faith. One of their legacies, one that still resonates in our culture, is revealed on the stones in early New England graveyards. With their sometimes inscrutable images, these stones provide glimpses into how these early settlers viewed this world and the next. Sermons, journals, and other writings from this period reveal a grim vision, and the gravestones' images reflect the same severity. From approximately 1640 to 1810, the craft of stonecarving flourished in New England, with hundreds of carvers producing thousands of works. Most of the stones still exist, their striking combination of beauty, oddity, grimness, and whimsicality available to anyone willing to search them out. Few people, though, will visit and view these underappreciated works of art, possibly because they deal so deliberately with death.

My fascination with early New England gravestones paralleled that of my brother, Bill, though for many years we approached the subject independently and from different perspectives, he through writing and I through photography. Each in our own way, we had always relished our time in these quiet, peaceful places. For me, the focus on the images of stone themselves brought me close not only to the human experience and expression of those early settlers, but also to a sense of meaning and expression in my own life. Often, in the end, what I have seen and attempted to record with my camera became more than I anticipated. When Bill and I discovered our parallel interests in these graveyards, we decided to collaborate on this book. I hope this documentary work pays tribute in some small way to the artistry of the early New England stone carvers.

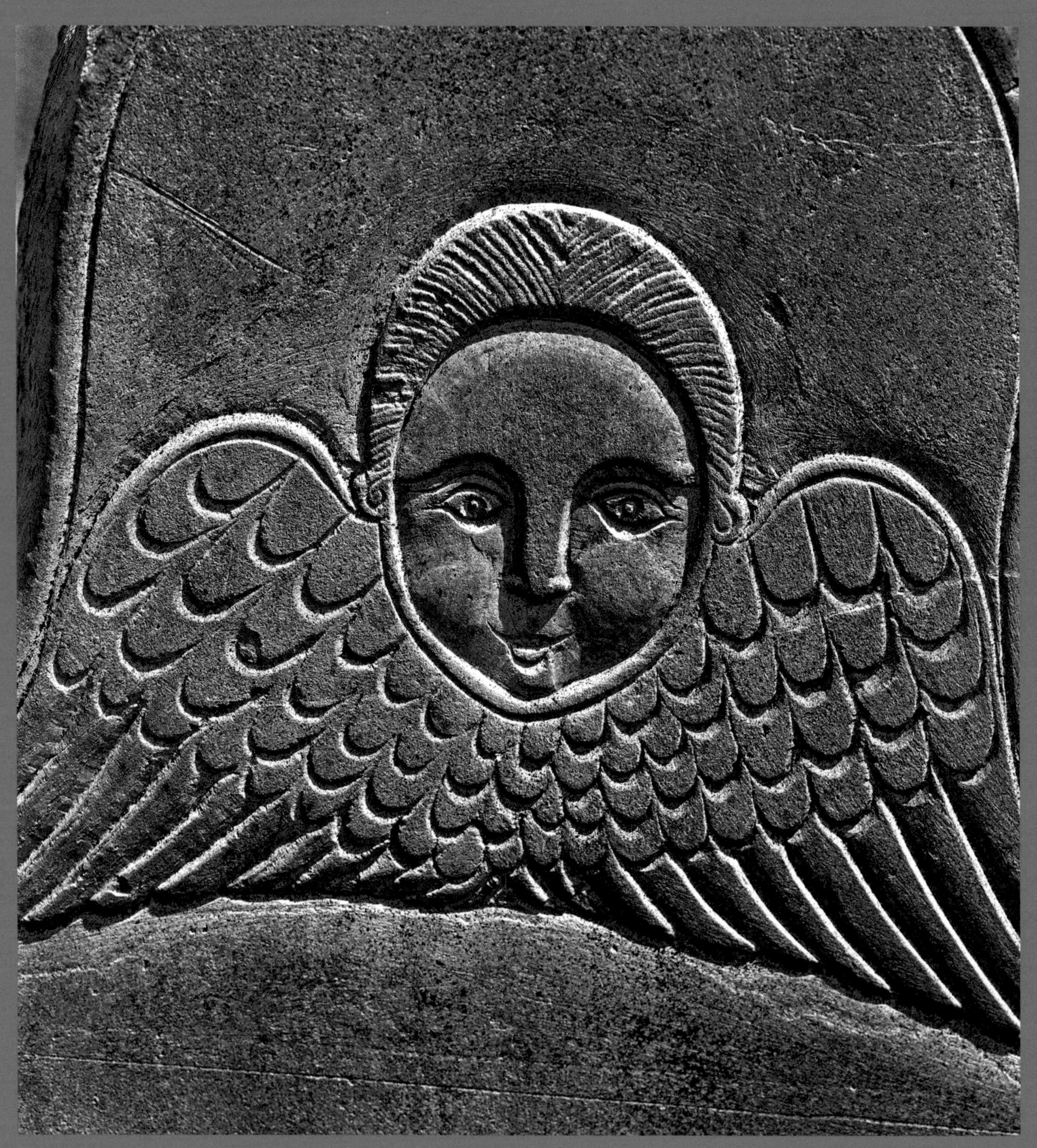

ACKNOWLEDGMENTS

For this book I am indebted to a number of people for their help and support. My heartfelt thanks and appreciation, in particular, to: Bob McCann for his careful and insightful eye and knowledge of all things photographic; Christopher Collins for his literary stylistic advice; Joan Schweighardt for her extraordinary attention to all details leading up to publication; Renee Rockoff for the preliminary book design; Suzanna Tamminen for her guidance; and to the many friends and family members for their generosity and encouragement, among them Judy and Noel Hanf, Juliet Taylor, James Walsh, Elizabeth Chan Reeves, Robert L. Reeves, Daria and the late Peter Hanssen, and Mary Coman.

Also, I would like to extend my gratitude to Jessie Lie Farber and the late Daniel Farber of the Association for Gravestone Studies for their extensive research and cataloguing of New England gravestones.

TEG

I am grateful to Carolyn Kuebler of the *New England Review* for her sensitive and careful editing, to the poet Keith Althaus for his numerous rereadings of the manuscript, and to Jeffrey Stern for his help with investigations of the Old Cambridge Burial Ground.

WG

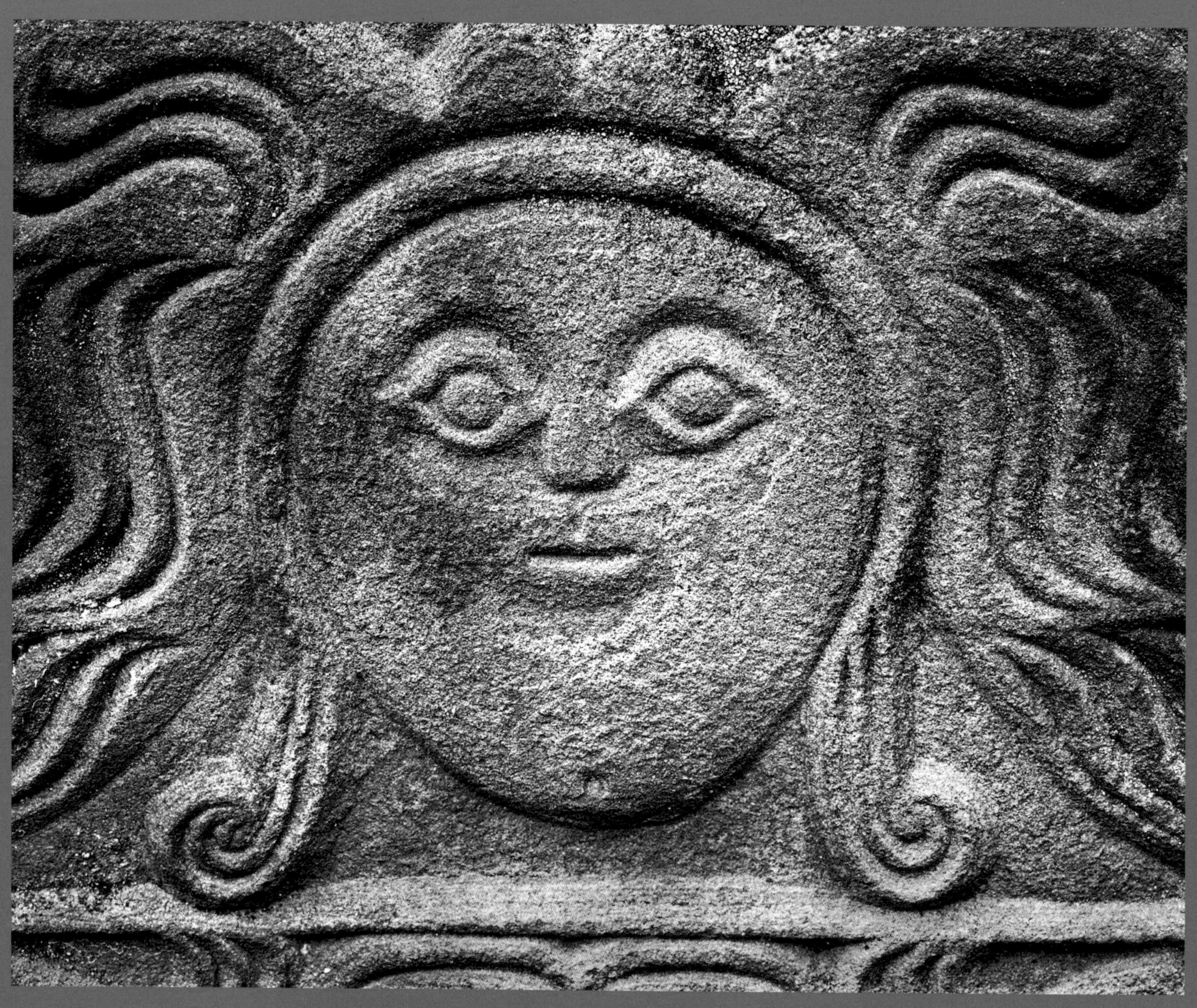

☼

STONE FACES

☼

Essay by William Gilson

☼

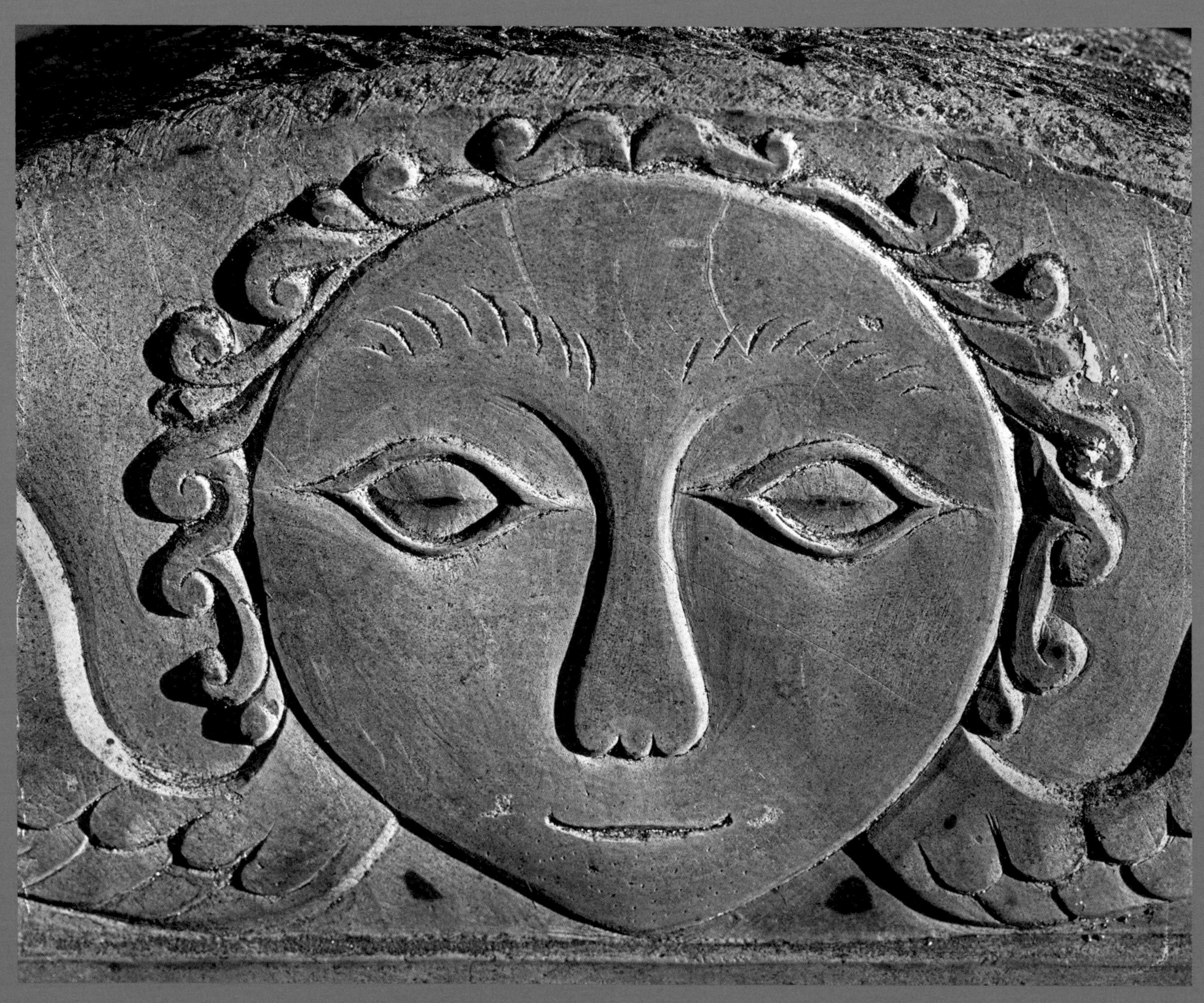

IN 1990 I LIVED in York, England. My apartment was about a mile north of the old city wall, and most mornings I would walk down Bootham, through the old gate called Bootham Bar, and explore the city. One drizzling morning, near Swinegate and Grape Lane, I came upon an archeological dig. Fifteen feet down, at the bottom of a hole about the size of a small living room, four skeletons lay exposed. Under a pale green tarp several archeologists in muddy clothes and colored hard hats were examining the bones, which had been carefully cleaned of dirt. The floor was level and free of debris and the skeletons drew sharp attention to themselves. One was a child, two were incomplete, and the fourth was an intact adult lying on his or her back with what looked like a small gravestone near the head. The bones of this adult appeared smooth, with a coffee-toned patina, and the skull looked to be grinning, the eyeholes large and round and dark.

I spoke with one of the archeologists, a young woman who seemed to be in charge, and she told me they had been digging "on our way to the Romans" when they came upon the skeletons, which she estimated to date between 1000 and 1100 A.D. She said the incompleteness of two of the dead was the result of a medieval wall; the intact adult had apparently been "an important person," as the archeologists had found signs of a wooden coffin. The headstone had two smoothed parallel surfaces but nothing could be seen to have been carved. The bodies were aligned on an east-west axis, heads toward west. The archeologist was blasé about all this, seemed a bit bored by my interest, and while we talked one of the team, who had been videoing the skeletons, began disassembling the intact adult, putting the bones into a large plastic bag. When I returned the next day, all the bones were gone and the digging was proceeding downward.

☼ ☼ ☼

I began liking burial grounds when I was a child. My earliest memories of them are too imprecise to allow of exact location, although I suspect they were cemeteries where my mother would leave flowers, places where members of the family were buried, old New England cemeteries such as the typically beautiful one in Middlebury, Connecticut, where my mother and father's ashes now rest under a small stone. I remember being told not to step on the graves, which caused me to notice the way some portion of the rectangle had sometimes *slumped*—a small thrill of horror when I pictured the person in the box down there, the weight of the dirt, the lid giving way.

On our annual summer trips to Ontario, to my father's childhood farm, on the long drives through New York State before the thruway was built, we stopped and ate picnic lunches. Sometimes we'd stop at a cemetery. Now, in my sixty-sixth year, with an accumulation of cemeterial experience, I can give context to those memories. Such places would have been pleasantly grassed parks, landscaped into levels with a variety of trees—maples, oaks, elms, ash, catalpa, various evergreens. Benches with wooden slats or cast iron vinework, facing modest but pleasant views. Gravestones, seldom aligned or closely spaced, made of white marble, gray or red or black granite, and ranging in size from small, plain, upright markers to tall gothics. Here and there a few large granite mausoleums resembling miniature Greek temples. Part of the appeal of these parks was in their quiet, their absence of people, the feel of safety; but mostly for me it was a powerful evocative oddness: the natural world of trees and birds and weather harmonizing with an underlying shapeliness, a shapeliness derived from something mysterious, at times scary. Everywhere I looked there were dead people, underground.

☼ ☼ ☼

In the 1970s I lived in Provincetown. I did a lot of solitary walking. One winter, feeling bored with myself, tired of sand dunes and of looking at the ocean, I discovered that for such a small place, Provincetown had a lot of acreage given over to the buried dead.

Some of my friends commented on the peculiarly large amount of time I began to pass in the cemeteries, but I grew happily absorbed. I decided I'd write an essay. A period of preparation was necessary, which involved spending much time musing among the gravestones, walking slowly about, and as spring came, sitting or lying on the grass, smoking, filling notebooks with scribblings.

Cape Cod is a peninsula mostly underlain with dirt and rock; near its end, beyond Truro, ocean currents have shaped sand into a huge hook that curls around a harbor. Provincetown lines part of the harbor, and if you walk east away from the town you come to woods and low scrub brush and sand dunes, and finally the Atlantic Ocean. Before there was a town proper, it was a stopping-off place for various fishermen, sailors, explorers, drifters; the town began to stabilize as a community in the eighteenth century. Always, until around the time just before I lived there, Provincetown survived by fishing for cod, mackerel, lobsters, whaling, whatever could be got from the sea. The nature of the land made that imperative, there was no way to farm.

The Hamilton-Gifford Cemetery, the Town Cemetery, the Catholic cemeteries (New and Old), the Oldest Cemetery—for a town with a permanent population of fewer than five thousand, there were a lot of graves, there was a lot of land that year after year had to be kept covered with enough grass to hold the sand beneath it from blowing away.

I got curious about the gravestones. They ranged from a few primitive markers, such as the imperfectly smoothed small gray stone in the Oldest Cemetery with the initials TN scratched with a blunt tool, to five or six nicely hand-carved gray slates, to many commercially cut and lettered white marble uprights and obelisks, to the standard modern ill-proportioned machine-made granites. There were a few small tombs with underground chambers, and a row of modest mausoleums set into a bank of sand. It was obvious from the proportionate numbers of stones and their dates that the town had had a period of prosperity during the middle and last half of the nineteenth century.

Into each stone was cut a name, or names, each with a death date, often a birth date as well; sometimes a quote or epigram. Seldom more. The lettering of some of the marbles—sharp-edged, well preserved in the clear air—now and then told of someone having been drowned, or lost at sea; one obelisk gave the latitude and longitude where a boat went down.

I decided to try and learn something about who they were, these underground old-timers. In a small room in the basement of the town hall was an archive. I got permission to squirrel myself in that room and became an almost everyday visitor. I made notes. Legal-sized yellow pages piled up. I read ledgers and odd slips of paper and old newspapers and Board of Health reports. What was I after? I said I was writing a book.

What comes back to me now are fragments of a half-imagined past, conjured through old-smelling paper, awkward prose, antique handwriting. A town where sand drifted between small houses. Windmills, salt works, huge outdoor racks of drying codfish, the harbor filled with schooners, the "mackerel fleet." A piece of paper certifying that old Seth Nickerson, whose grave I knew, had been declared senile; a woman—whose grave I also knew—was certified to care for him. Captain Mackenzie, climbing the foremast of his schooner alongside a wharf at low tide, got thrown off when the boat "keeled," he cracked his head and died. Another captain was returned dead from Suriname in a wooden coffin inside a steel box, packed in salt.

This period of "research," as I called it, ran its course, as did my time in Provincetown. No book materialized; I don't think I really was working on one. All my pleasure was in walking in the graveyards, in the reading and in the note-taking, disorganized and untidy as it was. I left in 1975, drove to the mainland in my VW Beetle, all my possessions, including my boxes of notes, in the car with me. Gravestones and burial grounds—what an odd lens to hold up to one's life. Two things retain a presence in my memory. The first was my discovery of New England Puritan stonecarving, which came about because of two 1745 stones in the Oldest Cemetery. The second was the smallpox graves.

❊ ❊ ❊

Smallpox. The skin confluent with acutely painful, pus-filled sores, eyelids swollen closed, burning fever, delirium. Virulently contagious. A 40 percent death rate, no effective treatment. Always lurking; epidemics came, subsided, then came again. There were two possible protections: vaccination and the disease itself. Vaccination was fairly common by the 1860s, but there were so many who hadn't been vaccinated and who hadn't had the disease that there was a ready pool.

In Provincetown a smallpox outbreak had killed an unknown number of people in 1801, and in the fall of 1872 it returned. Most likely by sea. One of the first cases went unreported by the attending doctor. New cases appeared. The old Pest House was in such bad shape that nurses could not be found to stay in it. The three-member Board of Health finally got things under control with quarantines and preventive enforcements, and in early 1874 the disease went away, having killed thirteen or fourteen people.

Someone told me about the graves in the woods, but not why they were there. I found them, after some poking about, amongst a dense growth of beeches and oaks and thorny vines. Instantly recognizable as graves, low-mounded, moss-covered, with small identical markers: limestone two-by-fours stuck upright, each with a single small sans-serif number. Maybe ten graves visible—it was impossible to be sure; some of the markers had been snapped off and lay nearby, some were gone.

Not far away was a hole about the size of a bomb crater, brush covered, with sloping sides. Maybe it was the cellar of the old Pest House; there was nothing visible to make this likely other than location. Trash from camping backpackers. An empty box of .22 shells.

A couple brief paragraphs and a list of expenses in an 1874 Board of Health report confirmed that the graves were those of smallpox dead. Nowhere did I find a key to the numbers on the stones, to who was buried where. It was promised that the graves would be fenced around and cared for, and it was recommended that the Pest House be rebuilt.

Here was a burial ground edging toward nonexistence: not because the dead were about to go away, but because the grave markers and the surroundings were ceasing to matter. In a subsequent visit I picked up one of the broken stones and put it in my backpack, intending to leave it at the local museum. I should have, but I never did. After moving it around with me for a few years, I last remember seeing it lying near a doorstep amongst weeds in Vermont.

An old story, marked graves becoming unmarked, a graveyard becoming normal land, the dead returning to dirt. During the ensuing years I've found that the memory of that place has stayed with me, has held some evocative presence that has never been displaced by the hundreds of burial grounds I have since visited.

☼ ☼ ☼

Provincetown was an unlikely place to discover Puritan stonecarving. Most of the gravestones were marbles from the nineteenth century, standardized imagery, weeping willows, funerary urns, patterns rigidly copied, no flair or eccentricity or feel of even a crude vernacular art. The pleasure was mainly in the cemeteries themselves, the expanse and the quiet numbers of stones.

But the Oldest Cemetery held two gravestones that offered something more; they were appealing as carved objects, very different from one another, each dated 1745.

One was the stone that marked the grave of Experience Rider. It was small—about two feet by a foot and a half—and close-grained, light gray, a single piece of slate most likely brought by boat from the mainland. About three inches thick, the back of it crudely roughed out, the front a hand-smoothed flat rectangle filled with lettering. The text was elegantly spaced, a handsome serif typeface:

HERE LYES BURIED
THE BODY OF
Mrs EXPERIENCE
RIDER WIFE TO
Mr *SAMUEL RIDER*
AGED 40 YEARS
DIED DEC.^{r} Y^{e} 21.st
1745.

Along the sides and bottom of the rectangle were narrow decorative bands of shallowly cut stylized long thick leaves, looking as if they were moved by a light wind. The top of the stone formed an upward curve, a third of a circle, containing the bas-relief frontal view of a skull with two large circular eyes, minimal nose, and grinning teeth; out from the sides of the skull projected a pair of wings. All of it had obviously been carved by hand, by someone working with mallet and chisel; cleanly done, but showing the small waverings and vagaries of an actual person working without machinery.

The other stone was that of Capt. John Tallcott of Connecticut. About half again as big as the Rider marker, a brownish red sandstone, somewhat abraded by weather:

Here lies Interr'd the
Remains of Cap.^{r} John
Tallcott of Glantenbury
in Connecticutt (Son to
Deac'n Benjamin Tallcott)
who Died here in his
Return after the Victory
obtained at Cape
Breton A.D. 1745
in the 41st year of his Age.

It too was roughly finished at the back, the front a text-filled rectangle bordered by bas-relief long-stemmed flowers and leaves at sides and bottom, and at the top not a skull but a face with wings: maximum simplification of line, two eye circles, a nose, a small mouth; wing feathers indicated by small half-moon gouges. Atop the head a small stylize crown.

In the spring of 1745, as part of the British-French hostilities then known as King George's War, a small army of New England volunteers had captured the French fortress of Louisbourg at Cape Breton Island. Perhaps John Tallcott had been wounded and died on his way home. Someone had gone to the trouble of having a gravestone, together with a small footstone, made for him back in his native state and shipped to Provincetown.

⁂

I drove south the length of the Cape, then north to Cambridge, where I planned to stay a couple nights with friends. I'd removed the rear seats from the Beetle, my belongings filled the back. I was on my way to northern Vermont. Behind the house in Cambridge was a small parking area and in the morning I came out and where the car had been were tire tracks in the snow that went out to the street. I had not unpacked the car. A few days later the cops found it, empty but for a two-volume edition of the journals of Henry Thoreau and the broken-off smallpox gravestone.

There was a period of adjustment. I kept feeling I was about to reach for something, then realizing I no longer had it. Socks, underwear, a precious stone arrowhead, a book, my extra glasses.

After some attempts to live and find work in Vermont I returned to Cambridge, where I settled for a watchman job, sitting nights in a small brick shack at the entrance to the old Watertown Arsenal, a mile of empty long dark brick buildings where tanks had been made dur-

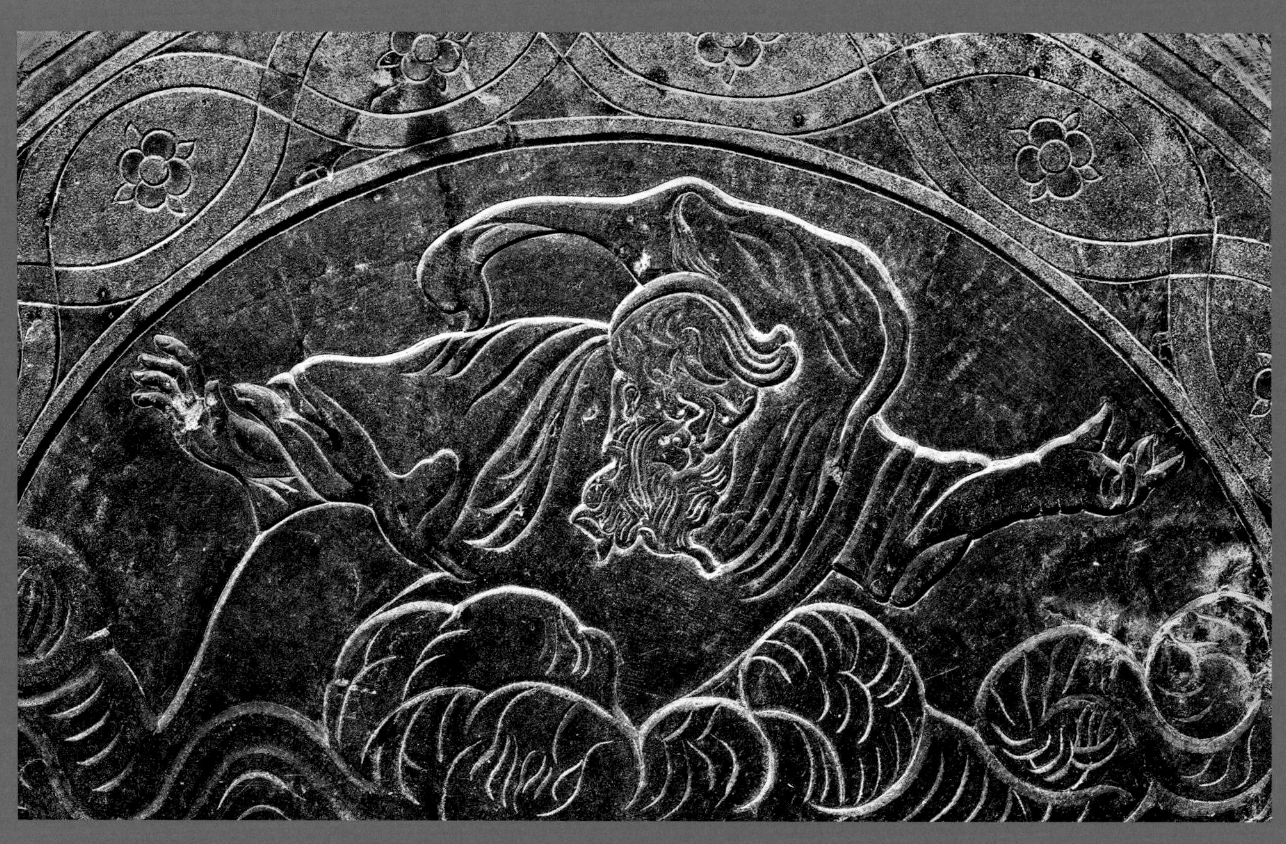

ing both World Wars. I read books and dozed in my chair, and during the daytime, besides whatever else I did, I began to seek out the old burial grounds.

☼ ☼ ☼

The first white people to settle in New England in sizable numbers were Puritans from England. Their religion, which many of them practiced with extraordinary focus and intensity, had its origins at least as far back as Henry VIII's split with the Catholic Church. The Puritans were not satisfied with the compromises resulting from that split, with what came to be regarded as the Church of England, and their pressure for further purification resulted eventually in the cutting off of King Charles I's head in 1649 and the installing of a Puritan government. But twenty years before that date there took place a migration to New England of some thousands, most of whom—and especially their leaders—considered themselves the purest of Puritans. They were intent on starting over, making a new state in what they perceived as a wilderness, where the word of God could be followed with exactitude, and the miasmic corruptions of medieval Catholicism forever boiled away.

First to make the crossing were members of a small, financially poor sub-sect of Puritans who came to be known as the Pilgrims. They settled in Plymouth in 1620 (after making first landfall at Provincetown). Ten years later the well-financed, well-planned "Great Migration" began, with shipload after shipload arriving at Boston. The natives—seen of course by the Puritans as heathens—were already by then dying of European diseases such as smallpox; here and there they made resistance but ultimately gave way as the Puritans went north, west, south, founding towns and churches.

These New England settlers were an amazing bunch. Aftershocks of their zealotry can still be felt in some of the crazinesses of modern America. They have been studied probably more than any other of the country's founding populations, and that is due in part to the voluminous wordage they left behind: sermons, diaries, histories, letters, civil records. In reading some of this material I have at times felt myself jerked without warning between dread and laughter. The intensity of their wild contemplations of sin and guilt and eternal damnation can seem, even to an unbeliever, at one instant as sharp as broken glass, and the next edging toward parody.

But to see them only as doom-crazed extremists of predestination and intolerance—as they have often been seen—is to make caricatures. The best of their writings are rich with thoughtful probings, extended reasonings, fresh metaphoric flights, eccentric perspectives, richly original language.

Certainly the audacity of Cotton Mather, beginning his *Magnalia Christi Americana; or, the Ecclesiastical History of New England*, can make a modern reader sit up and pay attention:

> I write the *Wonders* of the CHRISTIAN RELIGION, flying from the Depravations of *Europe*, to the *American Strand*: And, assisted by the Holy Author of that *Religion*, I do, with all the Conscience of *Truth*, required therein by Him, who is the *Truth* it self, Report the *Wonderful Displays* of His Infinite Power, Wisdom, Goodness, and Faithfulness, wherewith His Divine Providence hath *Irradiated* an *Indian Wilderness*.

Even allowing for the certainty of a shift in meaning during the past three hundred years of the word *Irradiated,* the choice of it still announces that Cotton and his God do not equivocate.

And consider the following:

Should I with silver tooles delve through the Hill
  Of Cordilera for rich thoughts, that I
My Lord, might weave with an angelick skill
  A Damask Web of Velvet Verse thereby
  To deck thy Works up, all my Web would run
  To rags, and jags: so snicksnarld to the thrum.

and

Lord, oynt me with this Petro oyle. I'm sick.
  Make mee drinke Water of the Rock. I'm dry.
Me in this fountain wash. My filth is thick.
  I'm faint, give Aqua Vitae or I dy.
  If in this stream thou cleanse and Chearish mee
  My Heart thy Hallelujahs Pipe shall bee.

These stanzas, each from a different poem, are the work of Edward Taylor. Born in about 1642 in England, Taylor made the crossing in 1668, graduated from Harvard in 1671, and that same year became minister to the recently incorporated frontier town of Westfield in western Massachusetts. He married twice, fathered fourteen children, served as minister as well as the town doctor until his death at eighty-seven. All through those Westfield years he wrote poems, which he never published, and he left orders that his heirs not publish them. The poems survived in manuscript, however, and in 1960 a complete text finally appeared—217 poems, revealing Taylor as a major American poet, certainly the greatest of the colonial period. Well-read and much influenced by George Herbert, Taylor had a style rougher than Herbert's but no less passionate. He combines intense, poignant longings for grace and salvation with a love of the world, its facts and textures. His language is eccentric, quirky, and in it I like to think I can hear something of what was to emerge a century and a half later in the personal vocabulary and phrasings of Walt Whitman.

One of Taylor's Harvard classmates was Samuel Sewall. Among the most interesting of the Boston Puritans, Sewall is justly famous for his diary, although during his long life he was a banker, lawyer, judge (he presided at the Salem witchcraft trials and later publicly apologized for it), town councilor, writer, printer. His diary covers fifty-six years, and to read it is to immerse oneself in the day-to-day struggles and pleasures of a likable and honest man, although every now and again the consequences of his Puritan rigidities of belief can be appalling. Sewall was intelligent and funny and flawed, and like his friend Edward Taylor he loved and feared a merciless God, continually studying His inscrutable movements.

Here are two of Sewall's brief (all his entries are brief) notes regarding the persistent problem of Quakers, whom Sewall saw as given to

"Devil Worship." The year is 1685 and Sewell is thirty-three:

> *Wednesday, June 17th* a Quaker or two goe to the Governour and ask leave to enclose the Ground [on Boston Common] the Hanged Quakers are buried in under or near the Gallows, with Pales: Governour proposed it to the Council, who unanimously denyed it as very inconvenient for persons so dead and buried in the place to have any Monument.
>
> *Wednesday, Augt.* 5. rode to Dorchester Lecture with Cous. Nath. Dummer; was kindly entertained at Mr. Stoughton's after Lecture. Going thither I saw a few Feet of Ground enclosed with Boards, which is done by the Quakers out of respect to som one or more hanged and buried by the Gallows: though the Governour forbad them, when they asked Leave.

These three characters—Mather, Taylor, Sewall—were contemporaries; they were not of the first generation, but they embodied much of the founders' fervor and certainty. During their lives change came to New England: here and there glints of an unseemly pleasure in moneymaking grew evident, discipline slackened, some of the moral boundaries revealed cracks; hard-line Puritanism began to experience its inevitable weakening. These three men, each keenly observant and articulate, from time to time expressed displeasure at these signs, sometimes with great passion; yet nowhere, so far as I can tell, did they show any concern with what was happening in the burial grounds, where stones marking graves had begun to proliferate, stones carved with imagery.

❊ ❊ ❊

I settled in Cambridge. I moved to a single room on Harvard Street, my home for the next fifteen years. All around, in Boston and surrounding towns, were the old Puritan burial grounds. Some were in bad shape, ill kept, littered, the stones chipped or broken or fallen. In some the gravestones had been taken up and reset in meaningless patterns. Others were nearly intact: one such was the old graveyard near Harvard Square.

The Old Town Burying Ground, between Christ Church and First Parish Church on Garden Street, is a flat, modest-sized enclosure across the road from Harvard, surrounded by high-energy traffic and big-money development. It remains, amazingly, a place where a form of simple direct contact with the old Puritan past can be made. There have been burials there since the 1630s, not long after the days of the first settlement, but the oldest date on a gravestone is 1653.

The backs of the old stones are roughly chiseled, in slanting light appearing from the rear as if recently quarried. There are neatly sawn marble upright slabs from later years but the older, more interesting stones are slate, some of them oddly small and massively thick. A few are plumb and level as when first planted, but three hundred years of settlings, frost heaves, rain and dryings have tilted and skewed most so that now a viewer sees a mixture of differing sun-angled textures.

Most of the graves are aligned east-west, with the headstone toward the west. The usual explanation given for this very old way of burying is that on the day of Resurrection the dead will rise facing Jerusalem. You can crouch down and peer closely at those stones, run your finger over a carved surface: this is not a museum, no guard is going to appear next to your shoulder warning you to stop at once. Feel the shallow relief of hand-smoothed stone, examine the strange pictures.

A slate marks the grave of John Watson, dated 1678. The top is a shallowly incised arch, beneath which sits a low-relief skull staring back at you. Not an altogether dead skull, though fleshless. Between two small, shallow, circular eye sockets is a nose made of three upward-tapering gouged lines: from these gouges two thinner lines continue, becoming eyebrows, each eyebrow curling at its end like a mustache twirl, giving the skull a touch of grin. From the edges of the nostrils sharp downward cheekbone demarkers touch two straight rows of teeth. The neck of the skull rests on a pair of joined wings, which rise up either side. The skull and wings together rest upon a horizontal rectangle containing small carved objects, symbols: a pair of crossed bones, a scythe, an hourglass, a coffin, a crossed pick and shovel. Above all of this, lettered into the slate in elegant capitals curving with the arch:

TE ESSE MORTALEM FUGIT HORA

I suspect that the oddity, the strangeness of such a gravestone isn't strongly apparent to most visitors to the Boston-area burial grounds (several are on the mapped tourist trails); there seems to be little surprise at such skull-and-bones grimnesses, perhaps the result of decades of fun-pokings at the dour Puritans. But to give the old stones some confrontational presence I like to imagine one of them magically transported to the newest section of a modern cemetery, where the last phase of a funeral takes place, the ceremony at graveside. The mourners walk from the car across mown green grass among polished nearly identical granite stones shaped like slices of bread. The names and dates on the stones have been precisely cut by firing a stream of steel pellets against a rubber stencil. Above an open grave, suspended on a chrome lowering device, rests a coffin of anodized pink aluminum. Just as the minister is about to begin his biblical reading, the mourners are startled by a loud low-pitched *whump*. At the next-door grave a strange stone has materialized, a thick low gray slate: on it a skull, wings emerging from a skinny neck, rises above a pair of crossed bones, and a voice from between grinning teeth screams:

YOU'RE ALL GOING TO DIE!
REMEMBER DEATH!

❊ ❊ ❊

Oof . . . bad taste, bad form. These stones are not jokes. Or is that true? Was there ever, at the subtlest level, a small laugh indulged as the carver carefully hammered tiny dings in the lower half of the hourglass, showing that all the sand has fallen?

When I saw a few Puritan gravestones, I wanted to see them all. The two that had caught my attention in Provincetown proved ordinary compared with what awaited. There are thousands of stones, and it helped that I liked old burial grounds generally, and that I liked traveling alone in rural New England.

Immediately upon beginning to seek out the old stones one becomes aware of the variety; it is not all grinning skulls, and even among that inviting genre there is variation enough to keep one looking for more. Patterns become obvious, geographic groupings, styles, runs of boring replication interrupted by startling displays of originality. Symbols bloom and replicate and die out, epitaphs undergo quirky modifications, the skulls become faces. What continues, until around 1810 when an entirely different approach to gravestones takes over, is the carving, the fact that a man (there are no records of women practicing the trade) is working with chisel and hammer, *by hand*, and even amongst tediously turned out copies one finds singular and curious pieces of work.

As an intellectual study, the big question of the Puritan stones is how they came to exist at all, given the nature of the society that produced them. The Puritans were iconoclasts; their religion opposed "graven images." This was not a theoretical matter: since the time of Henry VIII the Puritans had caused the destruction of vast amounts of religious art—windows, statues, rood screens, crosses, paintings. The smashings and burnings and cartings-off didn't let up until the restoration of Charles II in 1660. Yet twenty years after their arrival in New England those same Puritans began populating their burial grounds with stones inscribed with all manner of anciently evocative images. This paradox was never clarified by the Puritans.

One can enjoy the old graveyards, the beauty and variety of the stones, without getting extremely distressed by the knottiness of this problem. Any level of interest can be indulged within the pages of Allan Ludwig's *Graven Images*, where about a third of the book is given over to a meticulous examination of the particulars of the carved imagery. Ludwig argues that the imps holding arrows, hands extending from clouds, spinning rosettes, standing skeletons, reclining skeletons, cartoon faces, trees, crowns, dead children in coffins, strange, small, near-naked humanoids blowing horns—all of them photographed, described, located in the context of past appearances in Western art—are "symbols," not "decorations," and that they expressed for the people of seventeenth- and eighteenth-century New England fundamental truths that the formalities and codifications of their religion suppressed.

For myself, though I love his book and have read it several times, I find Ludwig's contention that to understand the symbols, and the gravestones, we must "see them as the Puritans saw them" not practically attainable. I'm still puzzled by the curious carvings, though I have looked at them again and again, in many places and in many differing weathers. My way has been to look at the stones first, consult Ludwig second, then follow out whatever further exploration of thought or road mileage takes my fancy.

❊ ❊ ❊

One of the difficulties of making sense of the old burial grounds is the seeming impossibility of paying sufficient attention, or homage, to the amount of pain and suffering represented. Pain of the dying and suffering of the grievers, the mourners. Among people who go to old graveyards it is common to remark on the numbers and death dates of children. Before modern medicines, many child deaths: sometimes most of the children in a family, sometimes all. Among the early slates it is not uncommon to find specially carved stones for three or more children; by reading the dates a story can be roughed out. Sometimes the mother's stone is nearby, her death date within a few days or weeks of the last-born's birth. But it is the information derived from the letters and numbers that gives the story, not the place itself. Even a cemetery that is uncared for, unpleasant to be in, will not come close to conjuring the actual grief and suffering. Each stone marks at least one death, its pain, dread, the moment approaching, watchers standing near, bearing the death in their own bodies, and then to go on living. Sometimes death is more benign than that—an "easy" death, perhaps a longed-for release—yet still it is death, still the awful chasm and the isolating loss. But somehow that is exactly what is missing from the old burial grounds. It takes work, it takes emotional and conscious and willful effort to bring it near, to—in the words of the old Puritans—"feel death's sting," there in the quiet and often beautiful presence of the place.

❊ ❊ ❊

There is a stone in the Phipps Street Burying Ground in Charlestown, Massachusetts, that I have revisited many times and, were I now living nearby, I believe I would go see it today.

You stand looking down at a low, very thick piece of slate, and it is a bit of a mystery, because it is double—as if two stones, each with an up-curving top, have been joined side to side; you expect two names, two burials, but there is just the one, and the inscription spans the whole face of the stone:

HERE • LIES • Y • BODY • OF • FAITHFVL
ROWSE • AGED • 74 • YEARS • DIED • MAY •
Y 18TH 1 6 6 4.

It is beautifully carved, all in capital letters of an elegant serif typeface, with a single suspended dot between every two words. The dots were common in this period before images appeared. There is a pleasing texture to this stone that augments its handsome solid proportions. Someone has shaped it but only so far; it is not quite symmetrically proportioned and it retains chipped indents and chisel marks, the finish having the feel and look of stone that has been much handled.

To me the lettering on this stone appears to have been carved by a man known only as the "Charlestown Carver." Although he didn't sign or initial his stones, his style is recognizable enough: he carved the John Watson stone, with its eyebrowed skull, in the Cambridge Burying Ground. At least fifty of his stones from the 1670s and '80s are to be found in Boston and surrounding towns. He seems to have been the person who transferred the basic gravestone form, as it had existed in England, to New England: rectangular area of text, arched tympanum with frieze below it, vertical pilasters at sides, horizontal embellishment at bottom. He established much of the basic visual vocabulary: especially significant are his finely articulated skulls, some perched on thin pedestals. He introduced small humanoid faces, fruited vines, discs, undulating leafage, and of course bones and coffins and picks and shovels.

But certainty in these matters is hard to come by, and perhaps it was someone else who first chiseled a crude coffin or skull on a now-vanished stone. I'm glad someone got the whole thing started. I'm also thankful for that quiet preliminary time when the Charlestown Carver—if it was the Charlestown Carver—made unadorned stones like the plain and elegantly lettered one for Faithful Rowse.

☼ ☼ ☼

James Lamson (1658–1722) is one of the Boston carvers who remains justifiably famous for his accomplishments in stone. Anyone wanting a summation of what this carver was capable of—as well as a memorable experience of one of the richest veins of New England gravestone art—should visit Wakefield, Massachusetts, to see the 1709 slate marking the grave of Jonathan Pierpont. Very little of the dressed front of this thirty- by twenty-seven-inch stone is left uncarved. Flowing wings lift a handsome skull, vines hang with imaginary fruit, small fat-bodied humanoids support palls that look like giant lips, two frontally posed Puritan preachers hold opened books, rosettes seem to spin alongside tightly clustering grapes and leaves and pendulous breastlike knobs. All this surrounds a generous expanse of elegant lettering that includes a long italic epitaph.

Lamson was one of the first, but very soon other carvers took up the challenge as population spread, new towns and villages made new graveyards. The highly inventive Boston styles filtered out to the provinces where craftsmen with sharp eyes and steady hands added their own touches.

The winged skulls evolved—or at least they changed by peculiar and not altogether understood ways into a variety of forms. After a while there were no longer skulls being carved, but several kinds of faces—round-headed ascending angels, simplified cartoonish soul effigies, abstractly geometric minimal mouth-nose-eyes, faces that today evoke Mayan death masks with electrically charged hair, sharply carved portraits of actual people, some minimalized, some realistic. And, accompanying the faces, all manner of symbology.

"Puritan gravestones" is a misnomer. The term is often used (as I have been using it) to refer to a relatively long period, from the last half of the seventeenth century to the first decades of the nineteenth—from the days when Quakers were hanged on Boston Common, through the Revolutionary War, to an America of more than seven million people with a Congress and a president and a capital city. Any persons still considering themselves Puritan by the end of that period probably would not have relished spending Sunday mornings listening to one of Cotton Mather's sermons.

With surprising suddenness the good carving ended. Gravestones bearing a weeping willow sentimentality, seemingly carved by machines and copied from pattern books, began filling a new kind of cemetery offering edifying views and tranquil walkways. The old stones went into retirement, appearing to most people—when they were noticed at all—as peculiar and embarrassing residues of a dark past.

It would be almost another century before the old stones were given serious attention: Harriette Merrifield Forbes, a photographer and writer, began motoring through the back roads and carrying her tripod and view camera into the burial grounds. She identified many of the carvers and sorted out their styles, and in 1927 published *Gravestones of Early New England*, an intelligent, congenial, down-to-earth guide, still valuable today.

☼ ☼ ☼

In the previous pages I've given the impression that I am not far from the places I have talked about. In fact, I am an ocean away, and have been for quite a while. The burial grounds and gravestones of northwest England are very different from those of New England, and while I have spent a lot of hours with my oldest son during his early years walking in a lovely nineteenth-century cemetery here in Kendal, my memories of the Puritan graveyards might have lost distinctness were it not for the work of my brother, the photographer Thomas Gilson.

I'm not certain which of us first discovered the pleasures of the old stones. Living for years as we did at opposite ends of New England, there were sometimes long stretches between meetings. I do recall one day at his house in Vermont looking through a pile of prints that had just come out of the drying rack and recognizing a Lamson stone with its characteristic finely cut teeth and wings. Having discovered a mutual taste for graveyard investigations, during the ensuing years we both kept at it, exploring individually and every so often traveling together to some acre of aligned stones, where Tom would set up his tripod, begin eyeing the light, while I poked about musing on the carvings and their surroundings.

When my wife-to-be, Alison, moved from her home in England to live with me in Cambridge, she showed a modest interest in old graveyards, and indeed trekked with me to quite a few of them. We traveled often in those days before children, driving around New England, New York state, south as far as West Virginia, and always I had my radar turned on, alert for the small fenced patch of near-abandoned family graves, or a quiet grassed nineteenth-century city necropolis with mausoleums and tall trees. Every now and again we'd come across Puritan stones—in Connecticut, red sandstone, cartoonish soul effigies similar to the Tallcott stone in Provincetown, or a soulful melancholy face cut with long, thin-drawn lines by John Bull in the 1760s in Rhode Island.

A burial ground in the New England countryside, and often in the city, is a place of quiet. Unless someone is being buried, there won't be many people about. There are usually trees, often old trees; and birds. If you like this kind of place, you will be thankful for the customs and attitudes attached to graveyards, however peculiar and delicately held they might seem. In cities and towns people will get drunk in the cemetery and kick over stones, and any frequenter of burial grounds will now and again encounter depressing messes; but by and large one can count on finding refuge, a nonviolent island of quiet and beauty, kept in place by the buried dead.

Some cemeteries offer nothing; the misery induced by a modern "park of remembrance," where all grave markers are flush with the grass so that tractors with gang-mowers can cost-effectively sweep, can leave you dreading for the future of the human race.

One antidote to such zones of blight, and antidote to much else, is to take a walk in Mount Auburn Cemetery, the 130-acre sepulchral park on the border between Cambridge and Watertown, Massachusetts. The first of the "garden cemeteries" in America, it opened in 1831, part of a European movement to bring the burial of the dead to the countryside, ending the practice of centuries whereby corpses were packed into small town and city graveyards that had run out of room. Mount Auburn was privately funded, well financed, designed and carefully landscaped with low hills and valleys, ponds, winding paths, curved carriage roads, avenues with wealthy mausoleums bearing street numbers, hundreds of marble gravestones unaligned on rolling grassed hills, grottoes and an abundance of trees and shrubs and floral intersections. The gates are locked at night, there are rules forbidding bicycles and picnicking, it is patrolled frequently enough to avoid vandalism. There is a paradox built into Mount Auburn, in that it manifests the essence of what replaced Puritan stonecarving and the egalitarian smallness of seventeenth- and eighteenth-century graveyards: it is the sentimental world of weeping willows and funereal urns and draped broken columns actualized in landscape, scaled up to become environment; it required upper class wealth for its founding and requires it still for maintenance; and yet it is a place of undeniable beauty and a delight and pleasure to walk in.

When Alison arrived in America and we began living together, one of the first places I took her was Mount Auburn. We bought some food on the way and in violation of the rules we picnicked in a little valley by a pond near a tiny neo-Greek temple, and later climbed Bigelow Tower with its circular stone staircase. From this highest point in the cemetery we viewed the winding course of the Charles River and the buildings of Boston and the distant hills to the west and north.

❊ ❊ ❊

Years later, I sit at a table in our house in Cumbria. It is the last day of September, sunrise several hours away, a steady rain falling. Upstairs, Alison and the boys sleep. Next to this notebook, a cup of coffee, and the latest pile of photographs from America, New England gravestones. When he sent them to me, my brother interleaved among the pictures several pages of quotes that he'd taken from various books of writings by the old Puritans, favorite passages.

A quote from Cotton Mather's *Magnalia Christi Americana*, where Mather retells an old anecdote about how one night in Boston a small group of men, "having inflamed their blood in a tavern," accost John Cotton, Mather's famous grandfather. One of the men draws near and whispers in the old Puritan preacher's ear: "Cotton," he says, "thou art an old fool." John Cotton replies, "I confess I am so; the Lord make both me and thee wiser, even wise unto salvation." This putdown, Mather relates, throws a "great damp" on the drunkards' "frolic."

It is interesting to have it so authoritatively affirmed that there *were*, in the days of John Cotton, groups of drunks staggering around Boston, and, moreover, drunks willing to indulge in the "frolic" of harassing one of the most revered stalwarts of the Puritan hierarchy.

The original New England Puritans, those of the first two or three generations, were half in love with death. You can't focus so intently on something, obsess about it with such flexed attention, without some part of you desiring it. Although the few descriptions that we have of the earliest Boston funerals tell of the plainest ceremonies—mourners silent around the grave, no talk, no eulogies—within a decade or two there had begun another of those examples of Puritan paradoxical behavior: funerals that look like celebrations.

The procession to the graveyard would be accompanied by tolling bells and would involve two sets of pallbearers, one to carry the coffin and one to carry the pall over it. Sometimes horses pulled the coffin and the horses were draped with black cloths on which were painted winged skulls, coffins, skeletons, hourglasses, "scutcheons." Handsome black cloaks were fashionable for these occasions. An invitation to the funeral often came in the form of a pair of gloves, the quality of the gloves varying according to the distinction of the recipient. Close friends or family might be given rings engraved with tiny skeletons. Sermons and eulogies were printed, and poems pinned to the coffin. Food was provided, rum was drunk. Samuel Sewall itemized the costs of a 1723 funeral amounting to about what a Boston schoolteacher got paid for a year's work. The general court several times tried to outlaw these expensive displays of funereal vanity. Cotton Mather railed in print against the rum-drinking and levity. Neither had much effect.

Whatever we may conclude about these strange goings-on, whether they were celebrations or peculiarly refined expressions of grief, they generally concluded, within a few days or weeks or years, with the placing of a stone at the head of the grave, sometimes a footstone as well. Carved into the headstone would almost certainly be a face.

Thomas's photographs are often of the faces. These range in time and geographical distribution from the earliest Boston skulls (let's assume a skull can be said to have a face) to the many fleshed-out variations that filled the graveyards by the beginning of the nineteenth century. Some Puritan gravestones are virtuoso displays of imagination and technique; others are simplified in the extreme, seeming to point toward modernist sculpture; but in most there is an unavoidable focus on the face: when you look at the stone, someone looks back at you. Who or what it is—Death? The departed? A soul? An angel?—is never made clear.

The faces look up at me from the photographs, and they are faces I love to look at. Many of them I have seen before, on the stones, out in the weather where they have endured for so long. But here they are something different, translated and held in another kind of permanence. Art from art.

For all the theorizing and study that have been devoted to the New England Puritans, I have never come across a convincing explanation of what was going on with the faces on the gravestones. By what route did they go from wild, teeth-bared, grinning skull to blob-nosed, lonesome-eyed cartoon? Are these images multiple ways of saying the same thing?

By filling the frame of the picture with a single face and thus removing for the moment all the accompanying symbols, and by patient and very careful attention to the sunlight, Thomas has made the faces appear as if caught in an instant of human expressiveness. Some flicker of emotion seems to be occurring, as if the creature in the stone is trying to make contact.

☼ ☼ ☼

The stones remain out there, stuck in the New England dirt, deteriorating as any man-made thing must, ultimately vanishing. They seem to have been made almost without thought, although that of course can't be. The absence of theorizings and documentation, and the fact that they appear to have violated principles of the prevailing religion, in the end only sharpen the focus of our attention on the stones themselves.

Allan Ludwig, summing up his massive study, says that New England gravestone carving, for all its glories, did not finally rise far enough above its "crude beginnings." In the rural interior an original vernacular art, still in its infancy, shaped by a native tendency toward functional simplicity (a tendency we see also in clocks, guns, ships), was swept away by a "great tidal wave" of nineteenth-century funerary urns, weeping willows, and toga-clad statuary. "It was the destiny of rural stonecarving," he says, "to remain only a whispered promise of what might have been."

I find it hard to imagine what might have been, where exactly the carving might have gone in a countryside of disappearing farms and pneumatic stonecutting drills. During the years between 1650 and 1815 a lot happened in New England, and all the while the carvers were tap-tap-tapping at the stones, and the dead, as they will, were quietly filling the graveyards. What we are left with is a great gift, a wide irregular distribution of patches of land of many sizes in which thousands of upright, doorlike stones mark graves that are aligned east-west. The stones are carved with all manner of odd symbols, with faces that stare at us angrily or sadly, humorously or inscrutably.

You never know quite what you'll find in those old boneyards until you go out and have a look. In southeastern Connecticut a wide expanse of stones, each with complex symbolic intertwinings and faces that seem to be trying to pull loose from their backgrounds. On a hillside in Vermont flat delicately dressed slates with the simplest of designs shallowly but precisely etched, sunlike disc-faces rising through clearest aether. Or a small clearing surrounded by hemlocks in New Hampshire, a few fieldstones, uncarved, next to a low crudely piled stone wall.

More than once I have been reminded that, after all, the whole earth is one big burial ground. Certainly the majority of graves are not only unmarked but unindicated, totally blended in to the details of land and sea. But this only makes so much more curious and worthy of notice the marked ones, the named and dated ones, the carved and aligned ones, those especially.

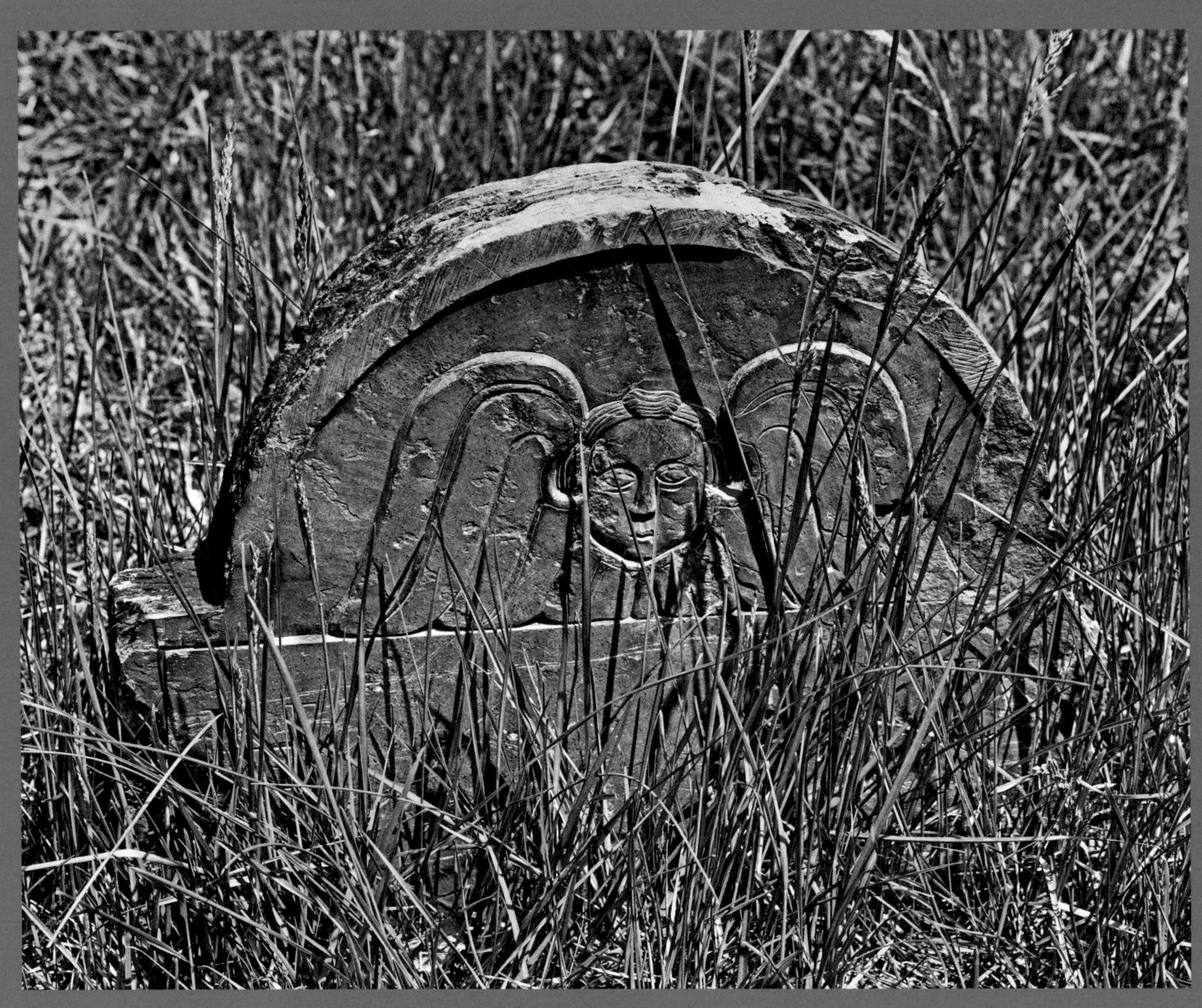

☼

PLATES

☼

Photographs by Thomas E. Gilson

☼

MATHEW

What may one learn by hearing the Cock to crow?

PRUDENCE

Learn to remember Peter's sin, and Peter's repentance.
The Cock's crowing shows also that day is coming on;
let then the crowing of the Cock put thee in mind of that last
and terrible Day of Judgement.

The Pilgrim's Progress, by John Bunyan

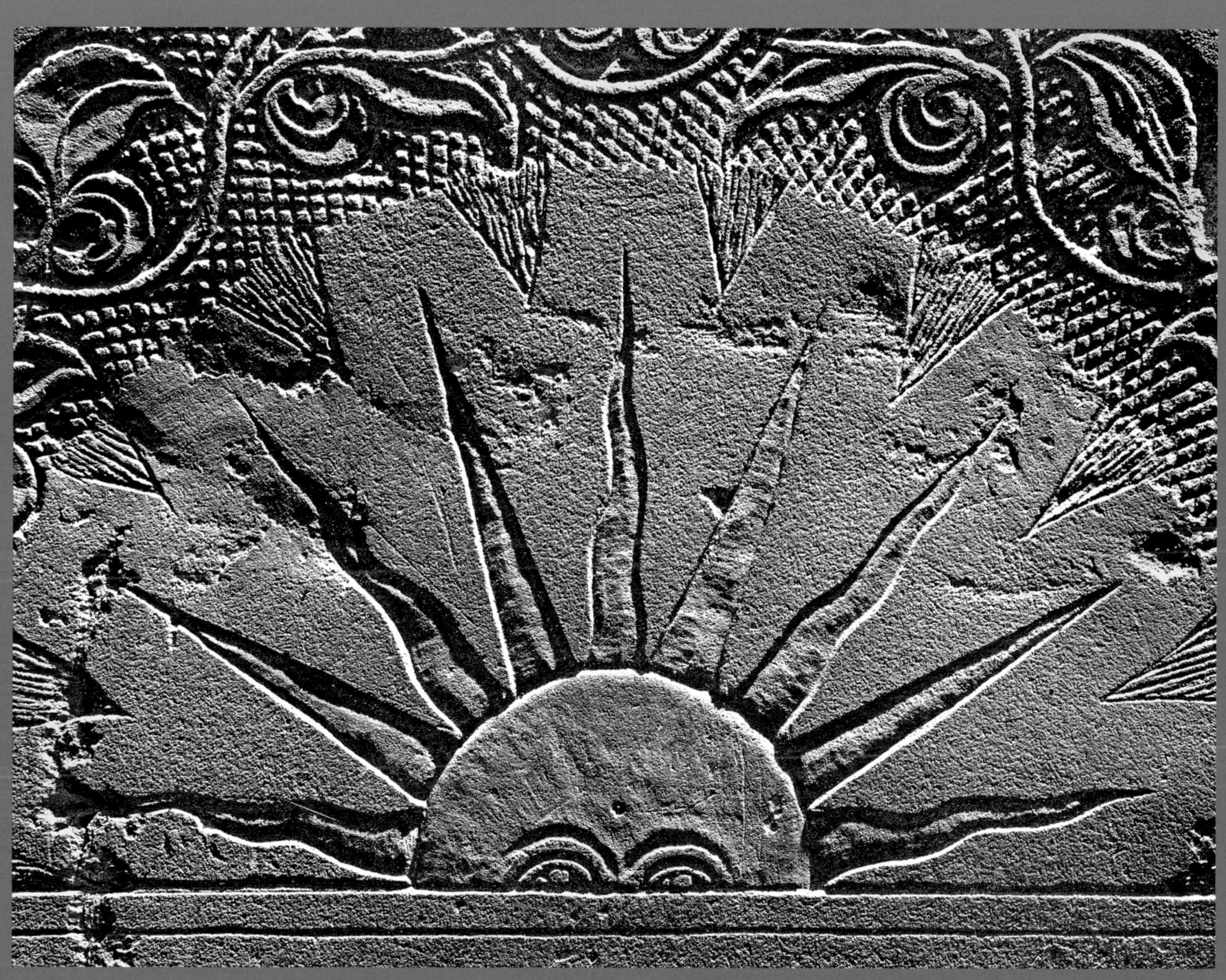

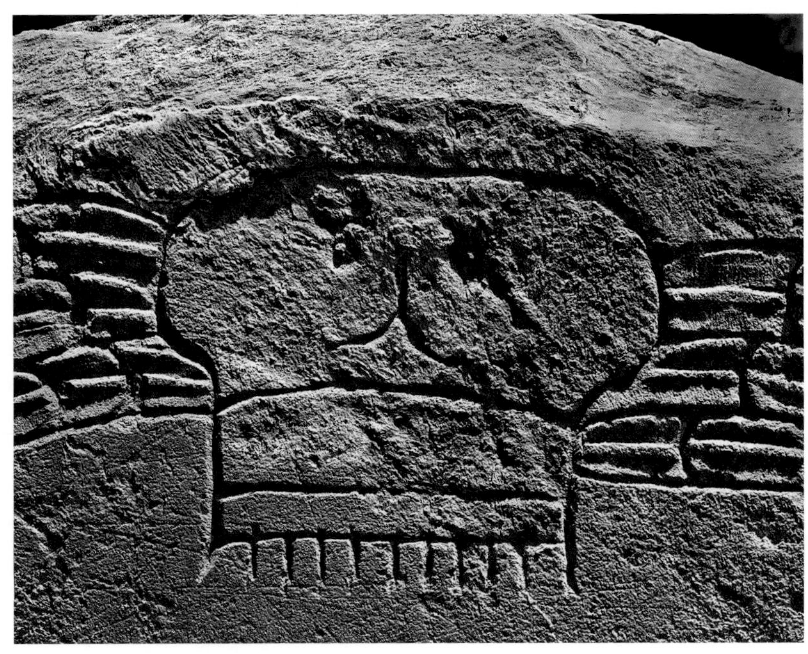

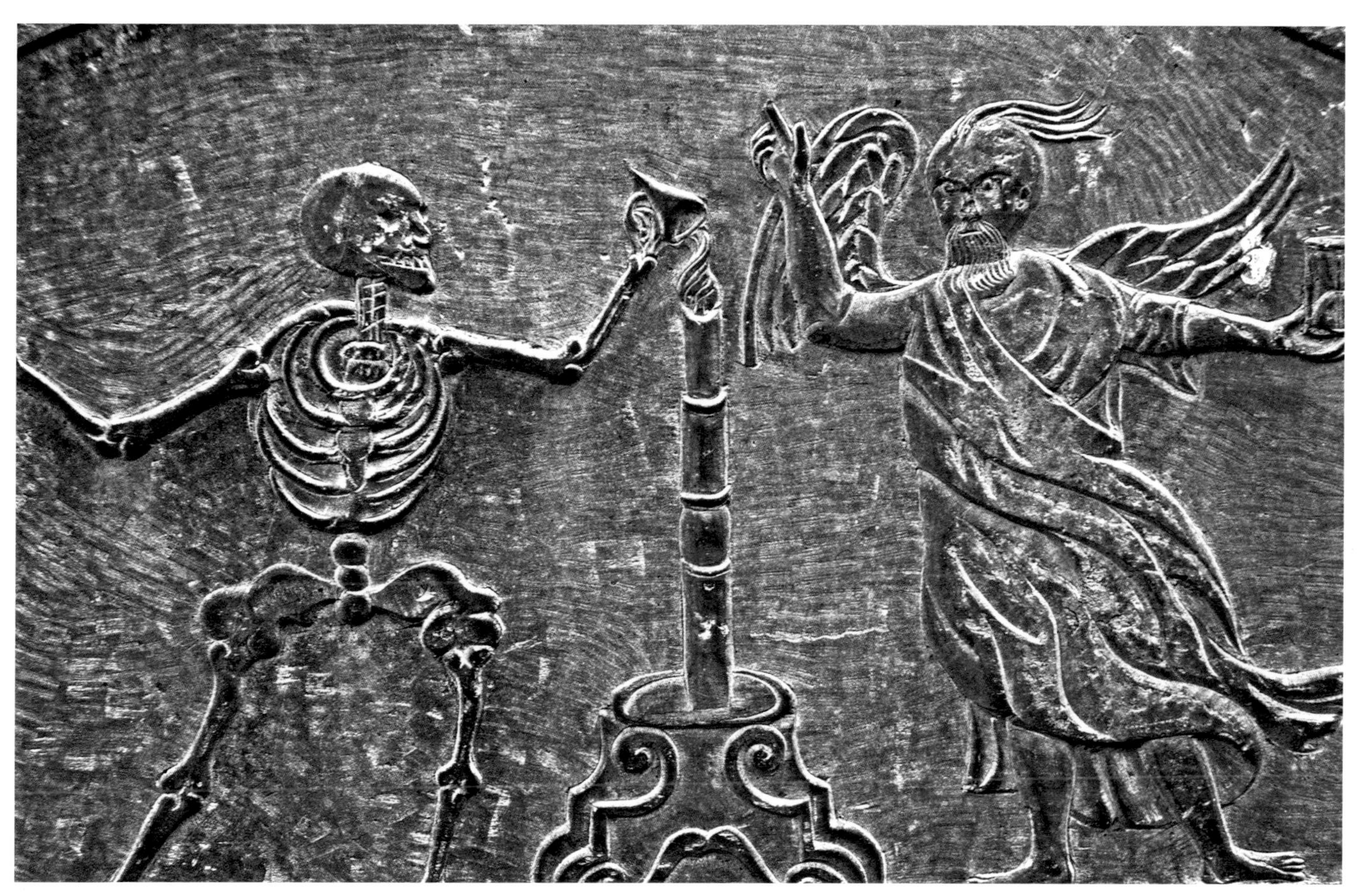

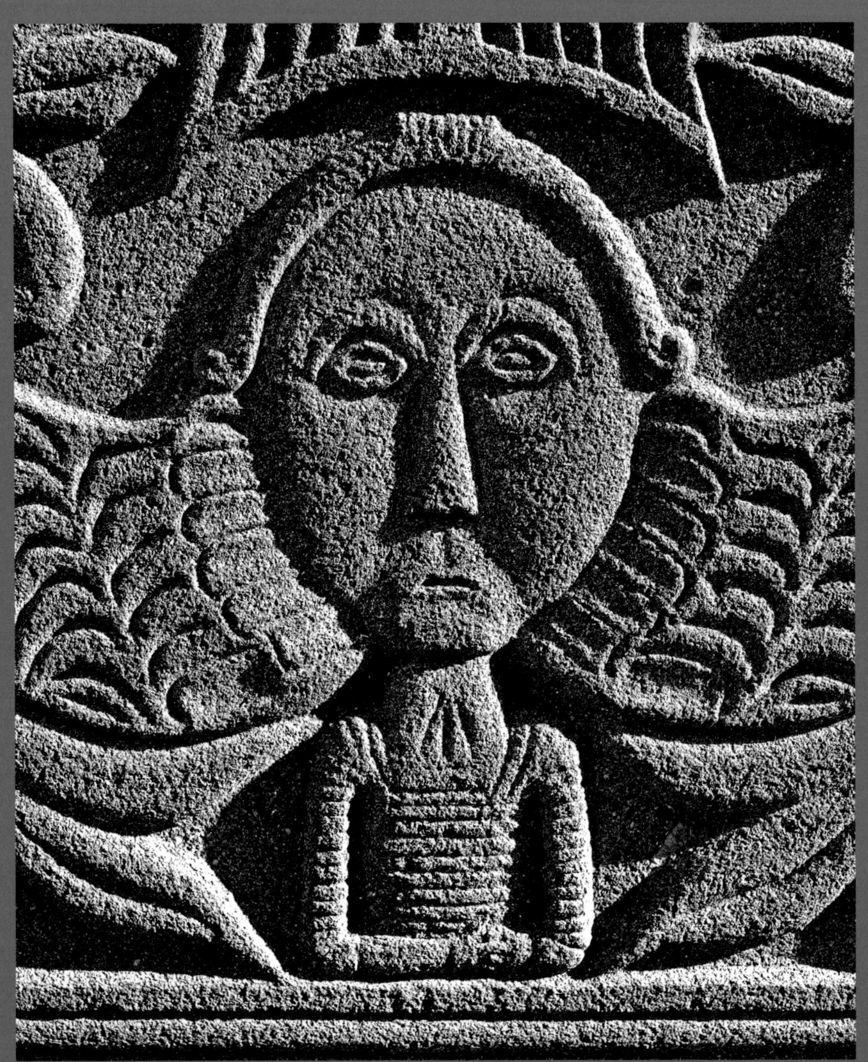

Having found a good haven and being brought safely
in sight of land, they fell upon their knees and blessed the
God of Heaven who had brought them over the vast and
furious ocean, and delivered them from all the perils and
miseries of it, again to set their feet upon the firm
and stable earth, their proper element.

Of Plymouth Plantation, by Gov. William Bradford

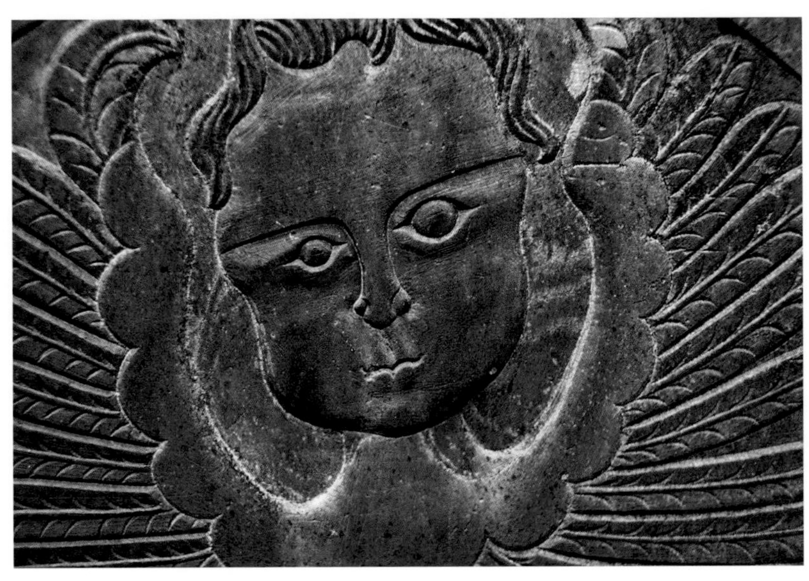

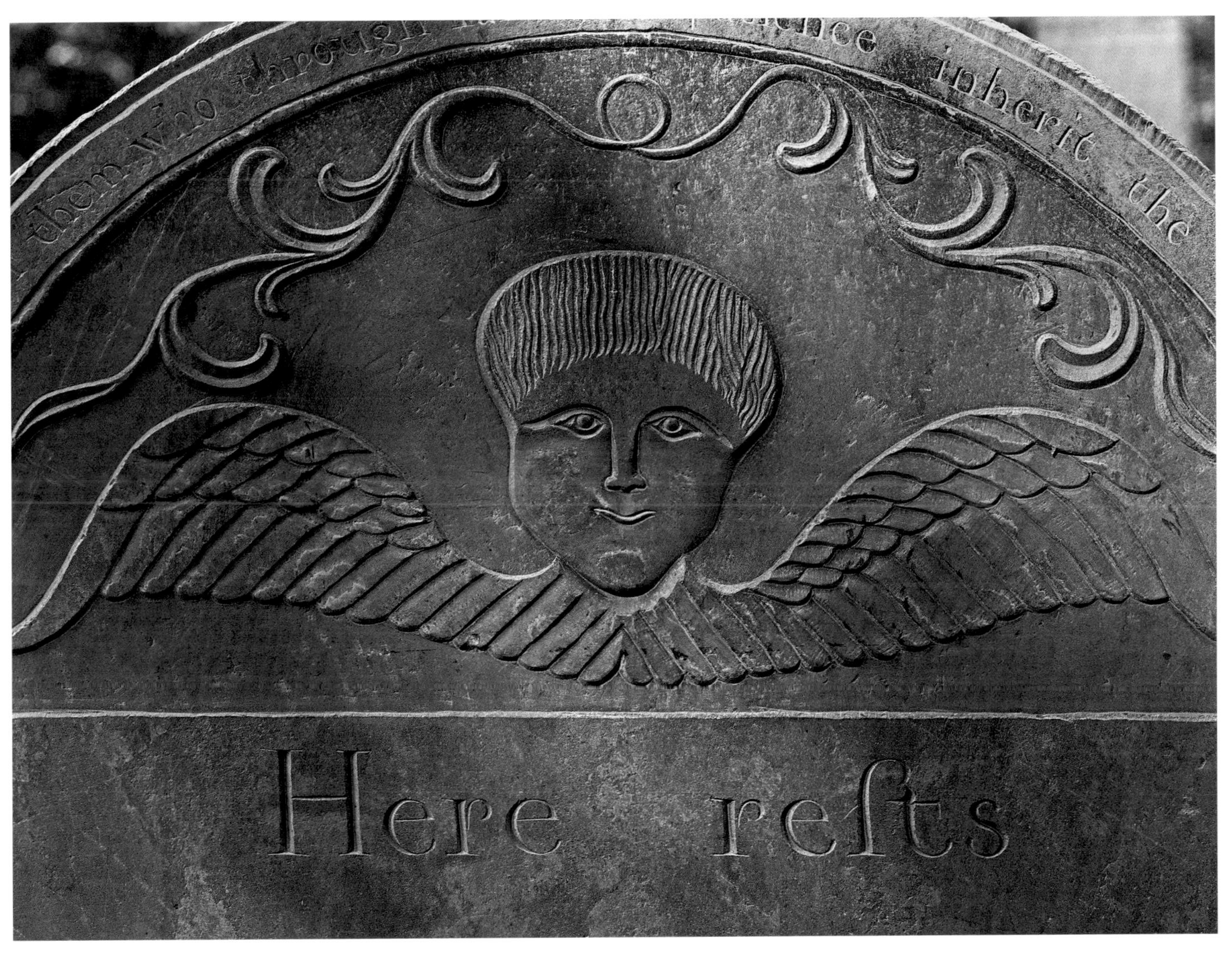
them who through
inherit the
Here reſts

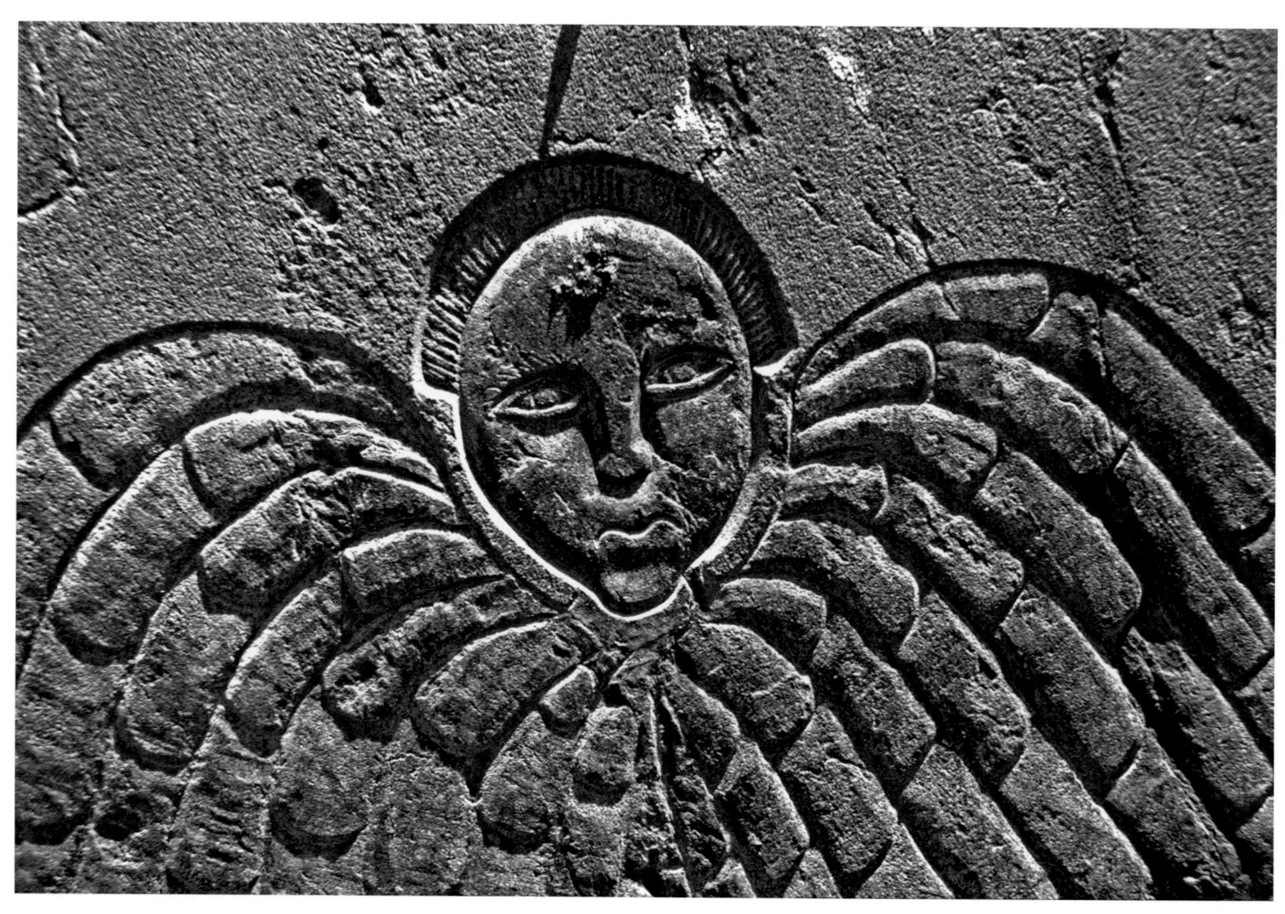

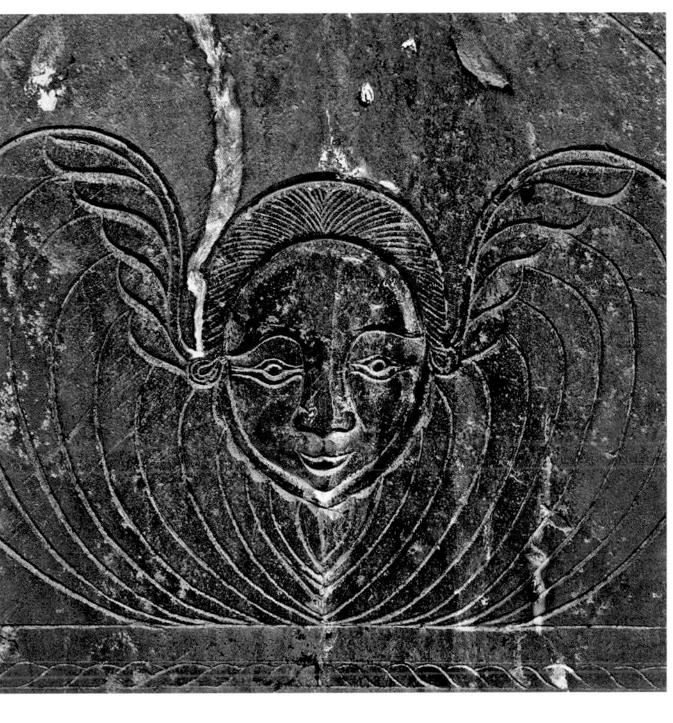

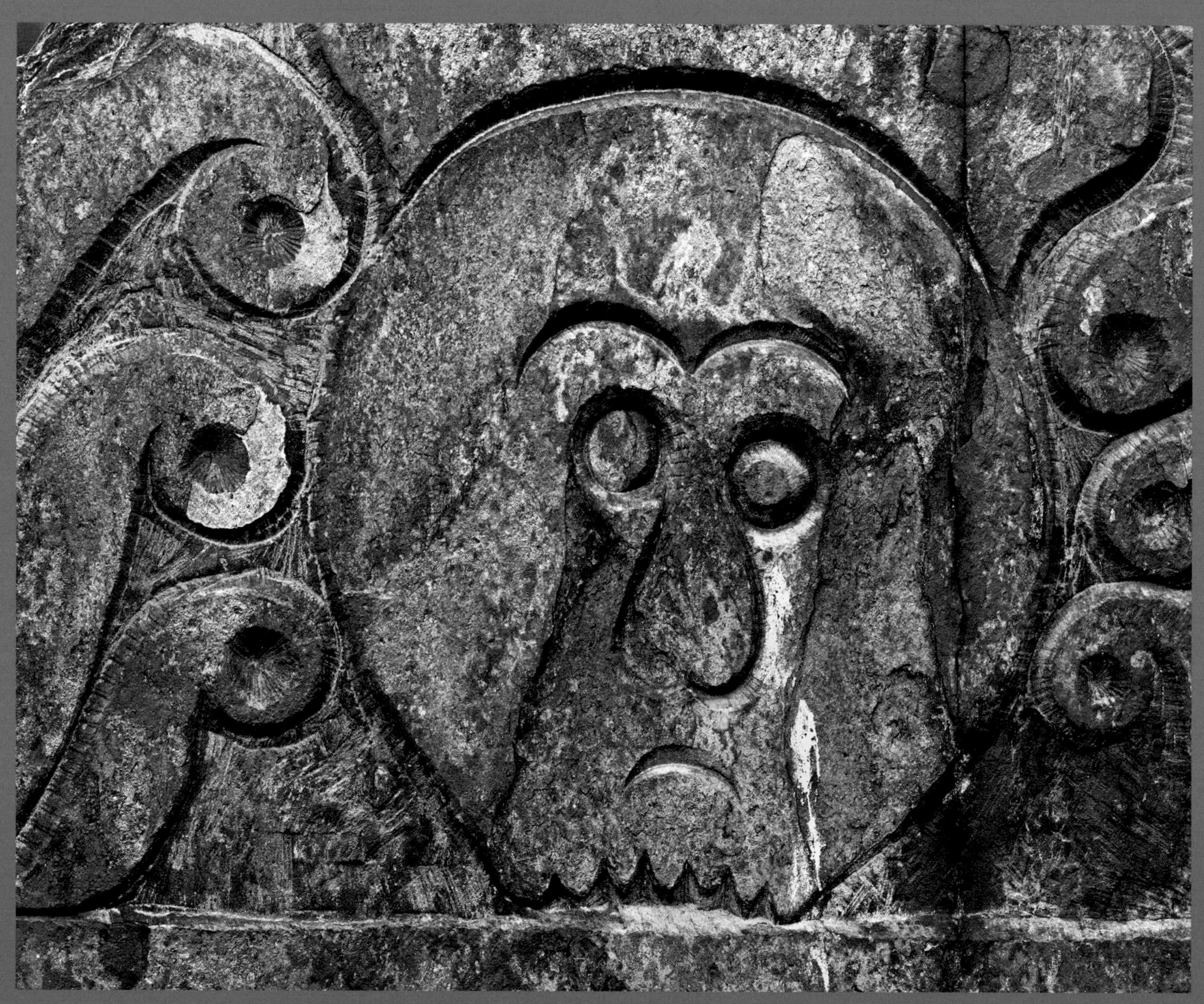

FIRST, be entreated to consider attentively how great and awful a thing eternity is. Although you cannot comprehend it the more by considering, yet you may be made more sensible that it is not a thing to be disregarded. Do but consider what it is to suffer extreme torment forever and ever: to suffer it day and night from one year to another, from one age to another, and from one thousand ages to another (and so adding age to age, and thousands to thousands), in pain, in wailing and lamenting, groaning and shrieking and gnashing your teeth—with your souls full of dreadful grief and amazement, with your bodies and every member full of racking torture; without any possibility of getting ease; without any possibility of moving God to pity by your cries; without any possibility of hiding yourselves from him; without any possibility of diverting your thoughts from your pain; without any possibility of obtaining any manner of mitigation, or help, or change for the better.

SECOND, do but consider how dreadful despair will be in such torment. How dismal it will be, when you are under these racking torments, to know assuredly that you never, never shall be delivered from them. To have no hope; when you shall wish that you might be turned into nothing, but shall have no hope of it; when you shall wish that you might be turned into a toad or a serpent, but shall have no hope of it; when you would rejoice if you might but have any relief; after you shall have endured these torments millions of ages, but shall have no hope of it. After you shall have worn out the age of the sun, moon, and stars, in your dolorous groans and lamentations, without rest day and night, or one minute's ease, yet you shall have no hope of ever being delivered. After you shall have worn a thousand more such ages, you shall have no hope, but shall know that you are not one whit nearer to the end of your torments. But that still there are the same groans, the same shrieks, the same doleful cries, incessantly to be made by you, and that the smoke of your torment shall still ascend up forever and ever. Your souls, which shall have been agitated with the wrath of God all this while, will still exist to bear more wrath. Your bodies, which shall have been burning all this while in these glowing flames, shall not have been consumed, but will remain to roast through eternity, which will not have been at all shortened by what shall have been past.

"The Eternity of Hell Torments" (Sermon XI), by Rev. Jonathan Edwards

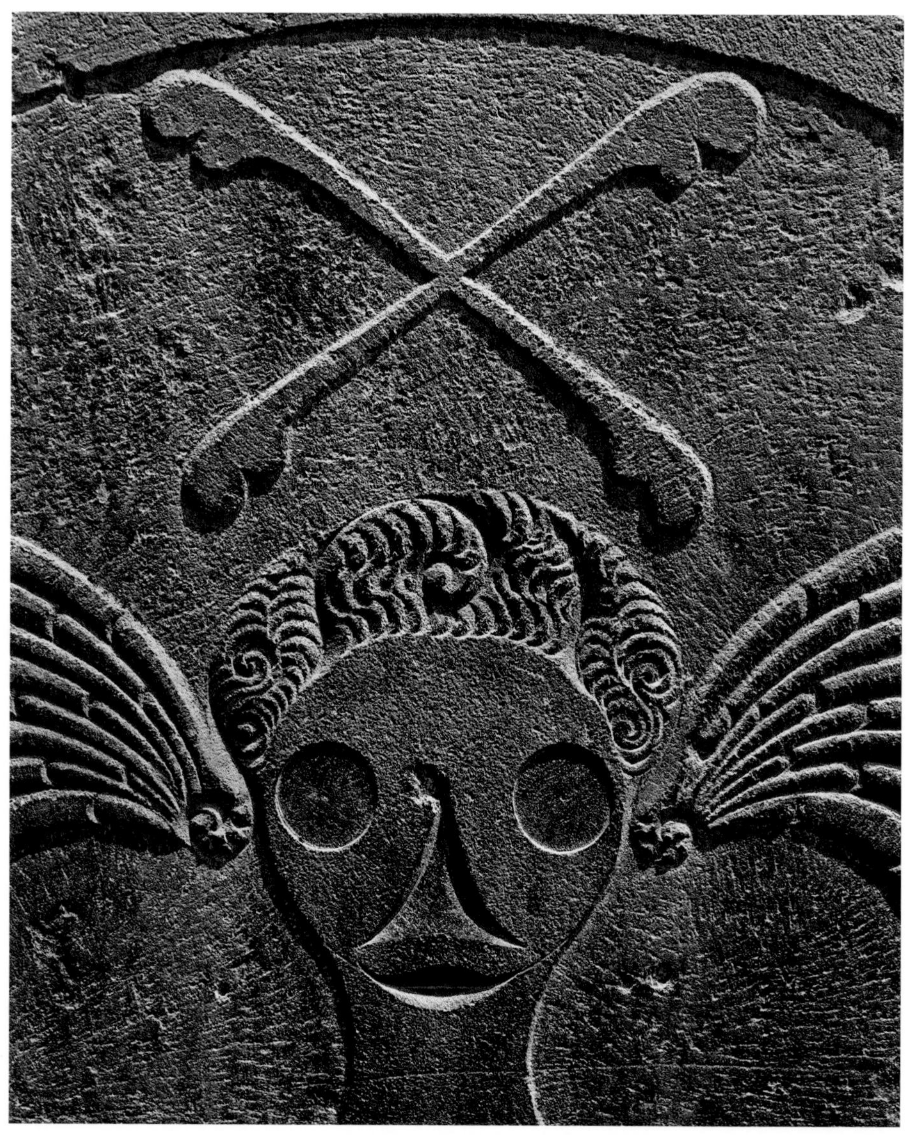

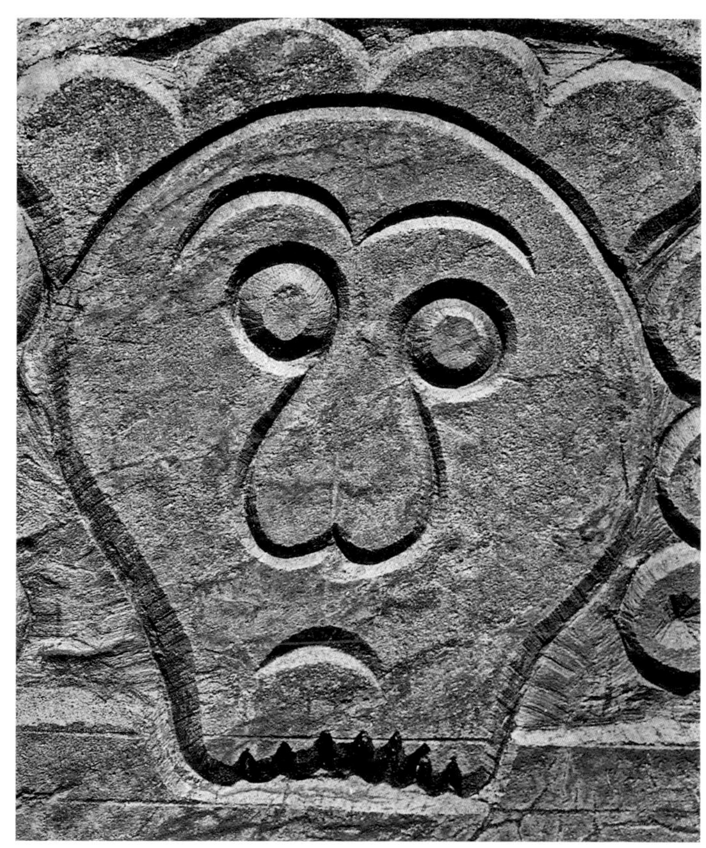

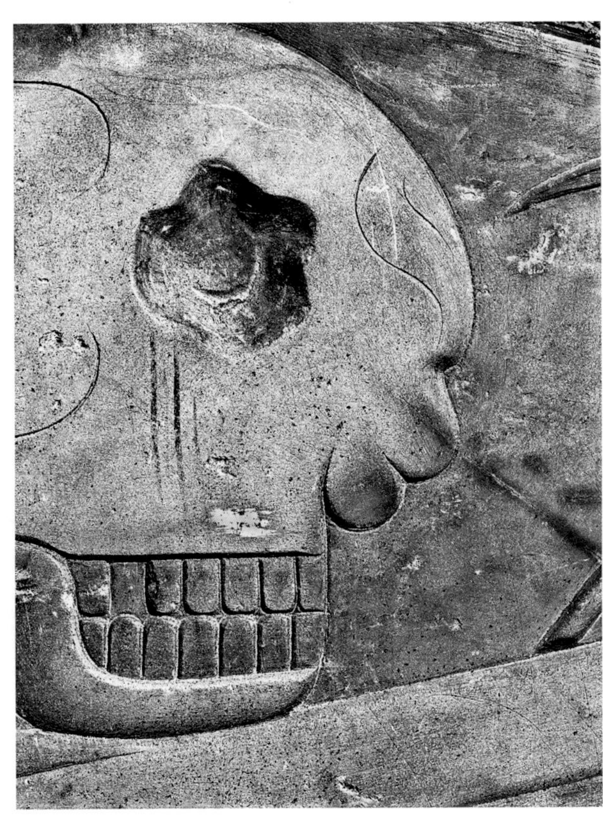

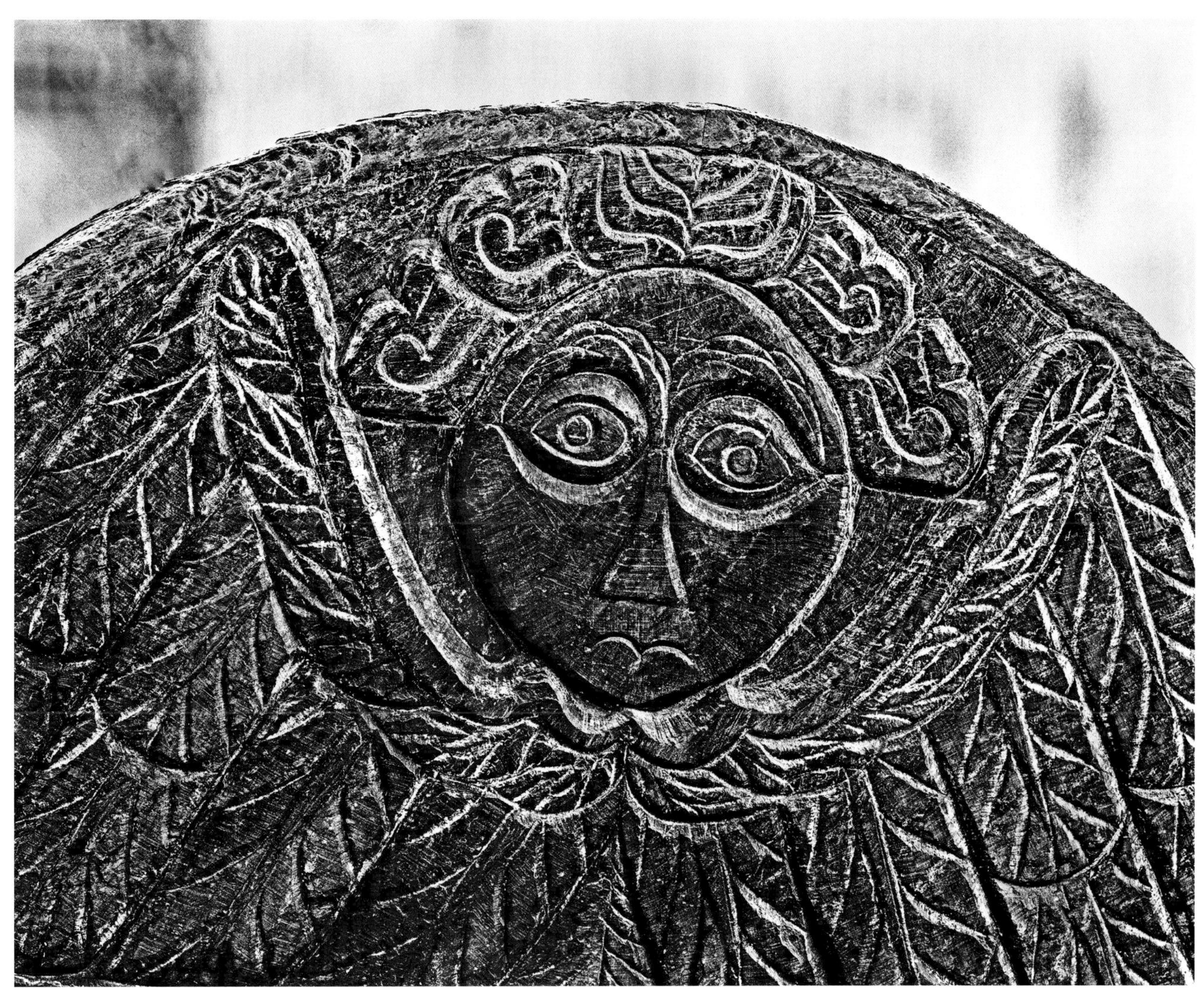

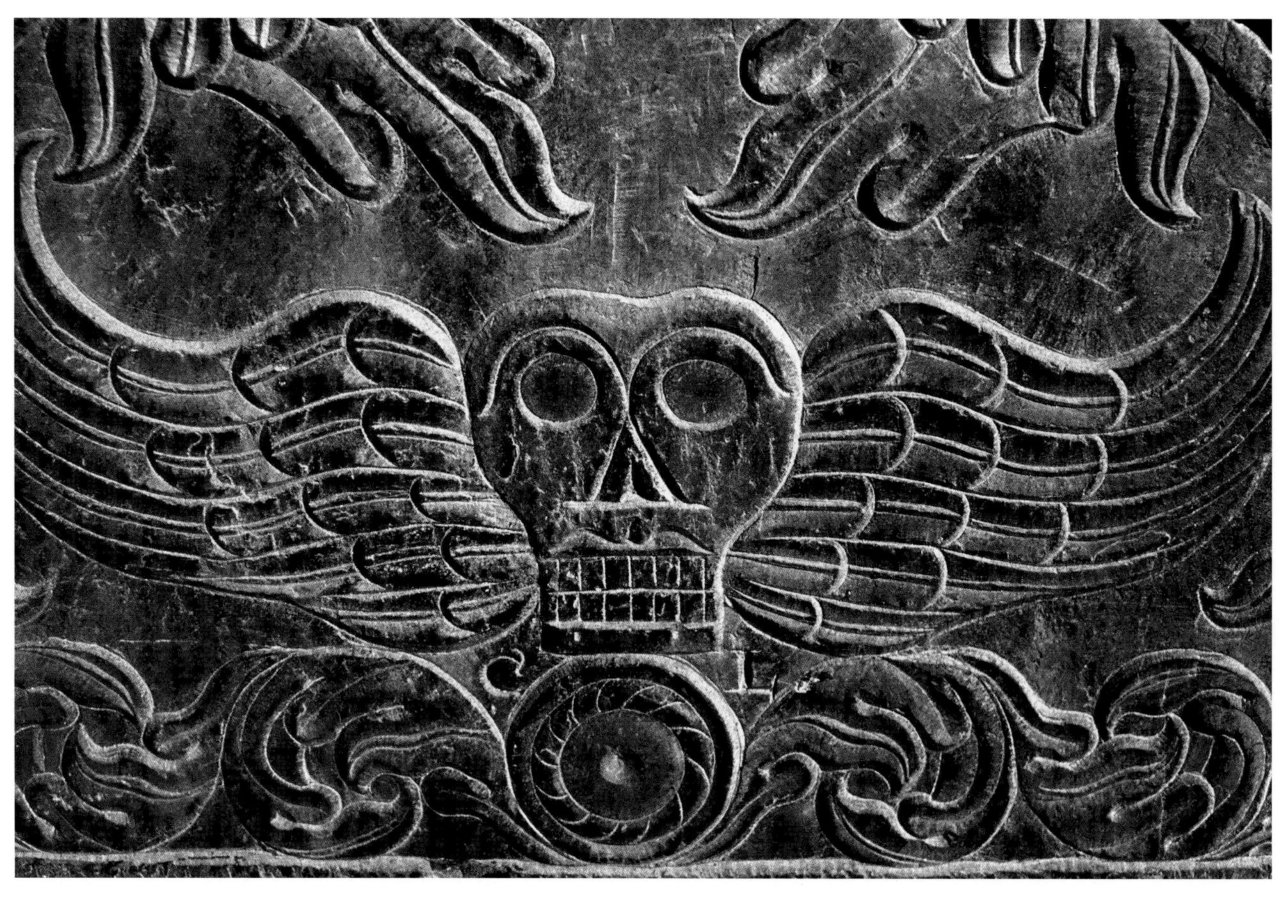

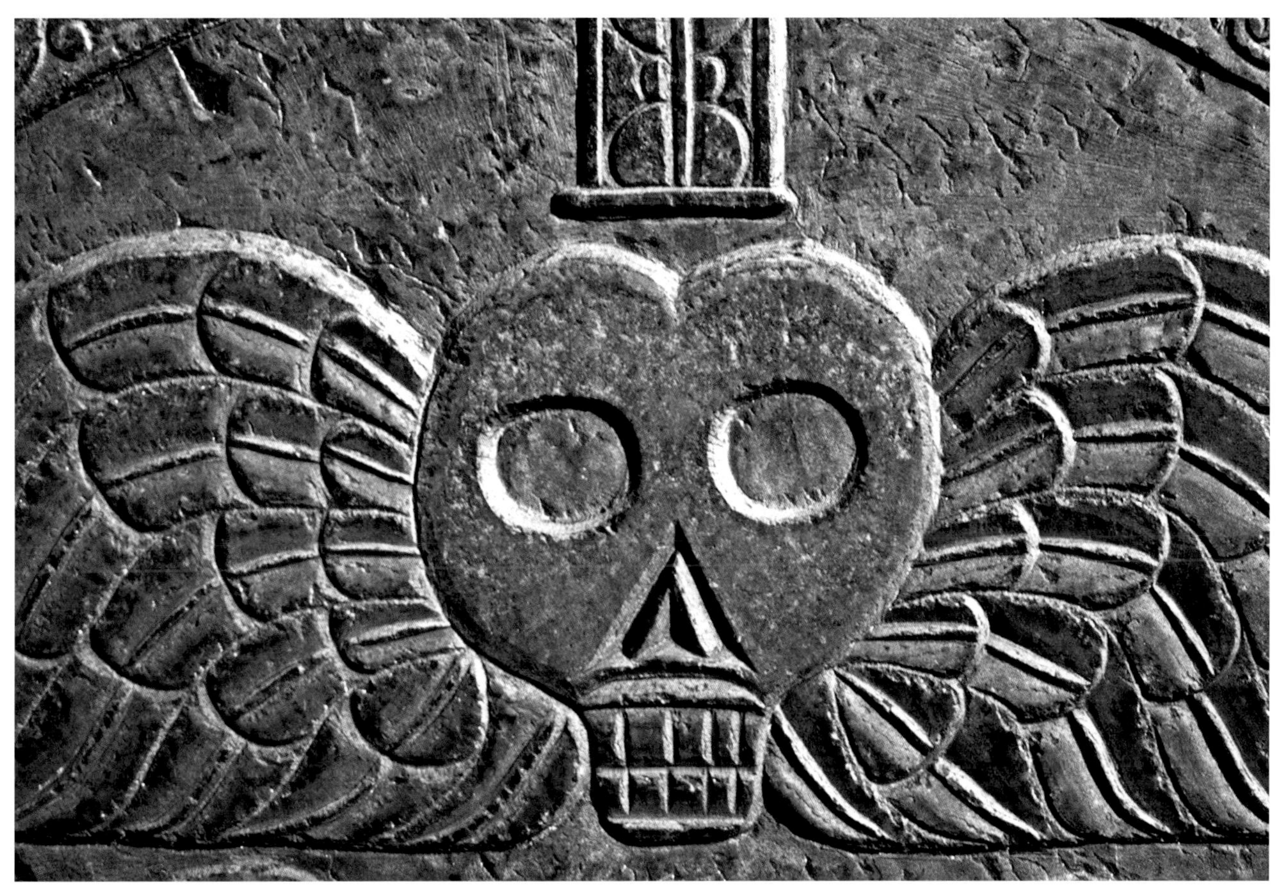

AUGUST 15, 1648.

The synod met at Cambridge by adjournment from the 4 (June last), Mr. Allen of Dedham preached out of Acts 15 a very godly, learned, and particular handling of near all the doctrines and applications concerning that subject with a clear discovery and refutation of such errors, objections, and scruples as had been raised about it by some young heads in the country.

It fell out, about the midst of his sermon, there came a snake into the seat, where many of the elders sat behind the preacher. It came in at the door where people stood thick upon the stairs. Divers of the elders shifted from it, but Mr. Thomson, one of the elders of Braintree [a man of much faith], trode upon the head of it, and so held it with his foot and staff with a small pair of grains, until it was killed. This being so remarkable, and nothing falling out but by divine providence, it is out of doubt, the Lord discovered somewhat of His mind in it. The serpent is the devil; the synod, the representative of the churches of Christ in New England. The devil had formerly and lately attempted their disturbance and dissolution; but their faith in the seed of the woman overcame him and crushed his head.

Journal of John Winthrop

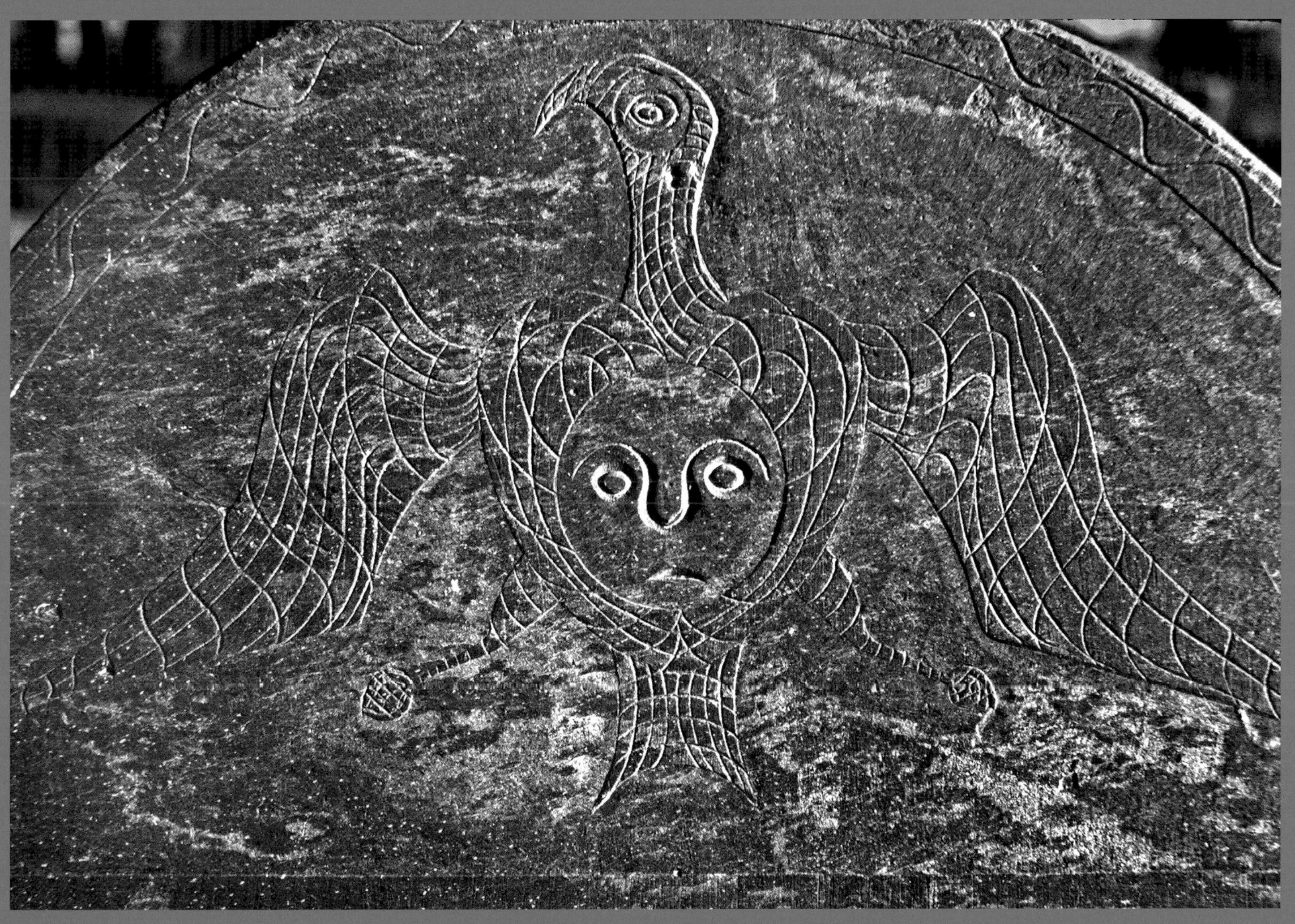

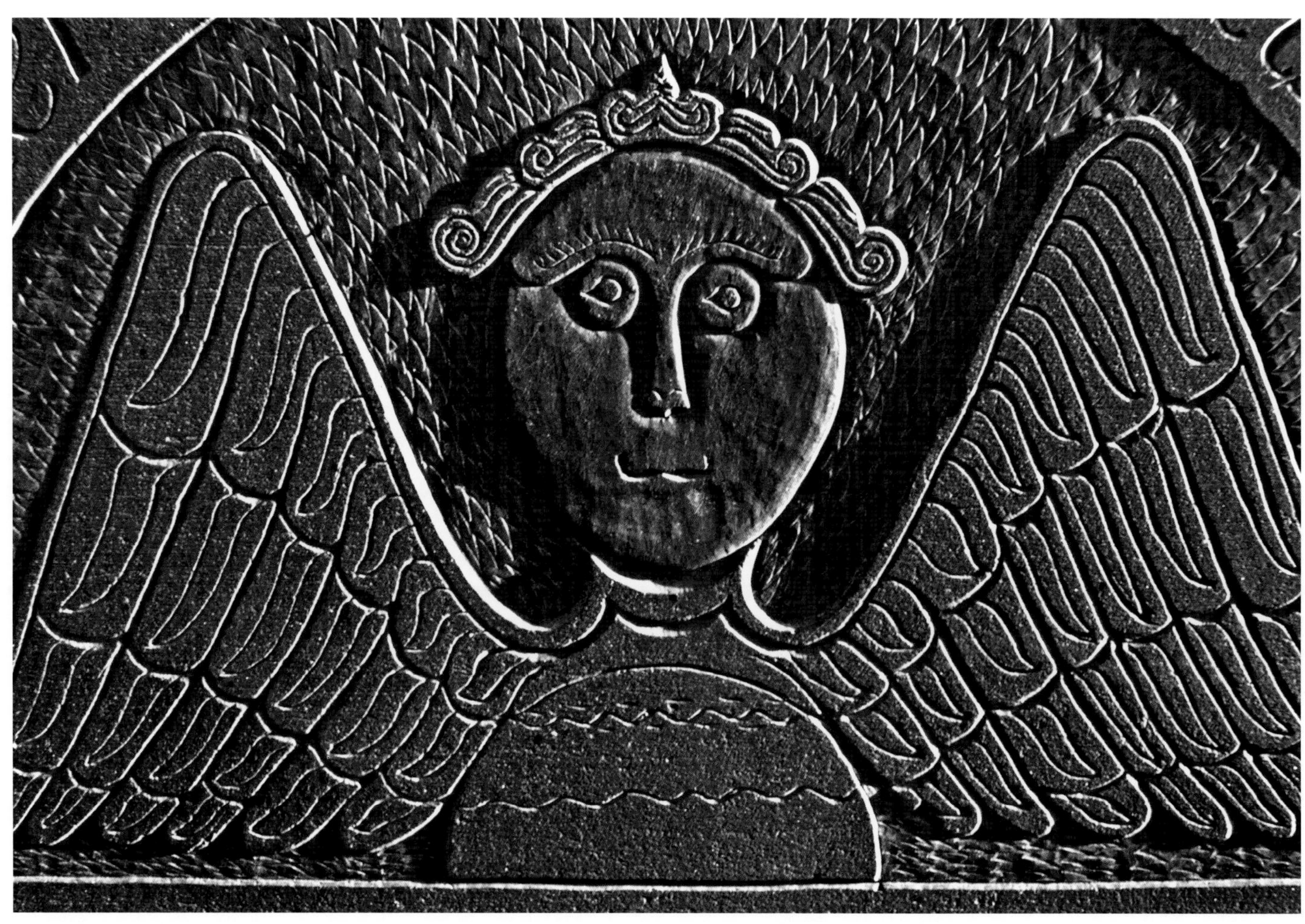

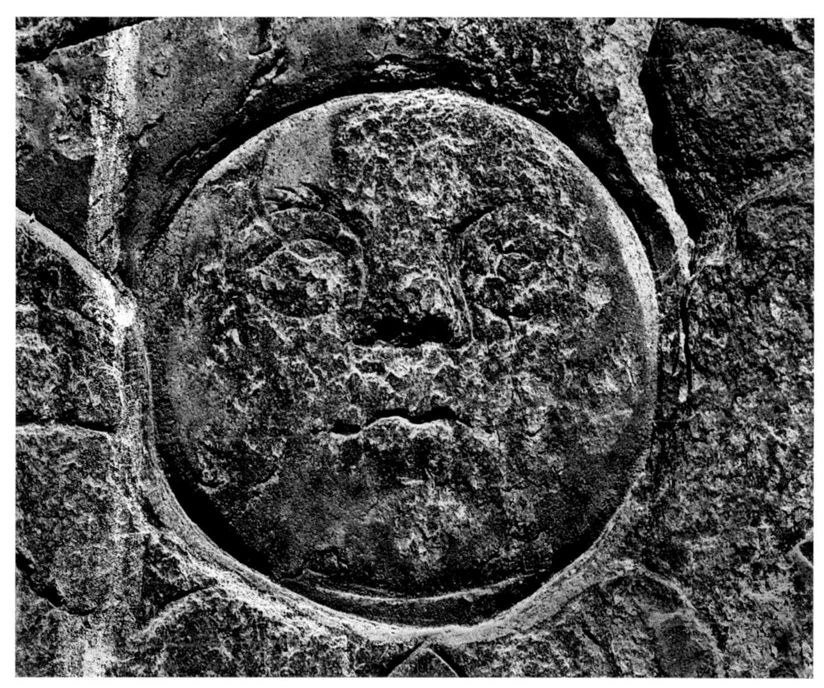

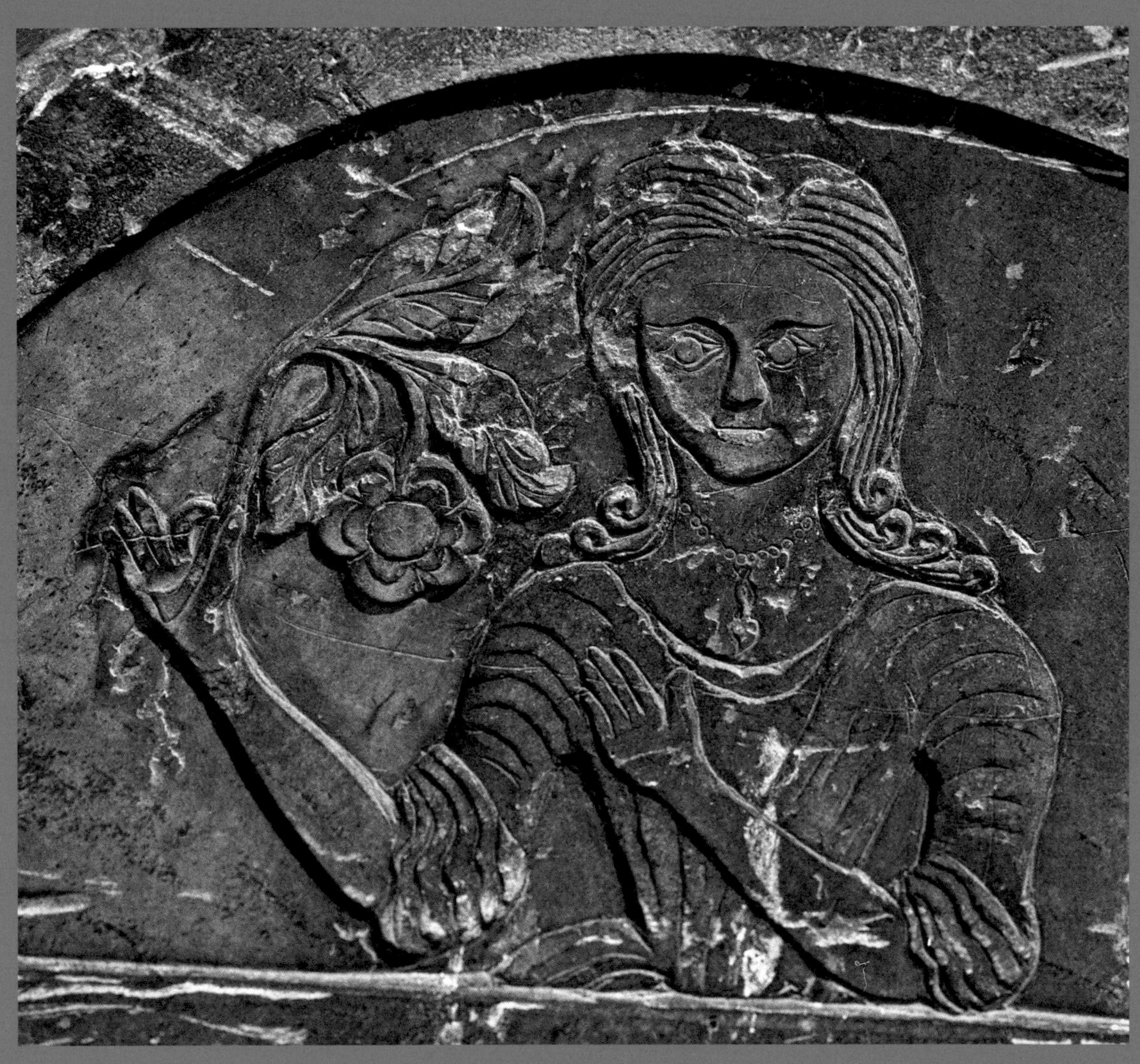

[APRIL 13, 1645.]

Mr. Hopkins, The Governor of Hartford upon Connecticut, came to Boston, and brought his wife with him (a godly young woman, and of special parts), who was fallen into a sad infirmity, the loss of her understanding and reason, which had been growing upon her divers years, by occasion of her giving herself wholly to reading and writing, and had written many books. Her husband, being very loving and tender of her, was loath to grieve her; but he saw his error, when it was too late. For if she had tended her household affairs, and such things as belong to women and not gone out of her way and calling to meddle in such things as are proper for men, whose minds are stronger, etc. she had kept her wits, and might have improved them usefully and honorably in the place God had set her. He brought her to Boston, and left her with her brother, one Mr. Yale, a merchant, to try what means might be had here for her. But no help could be had.

Journal of John Winthrop

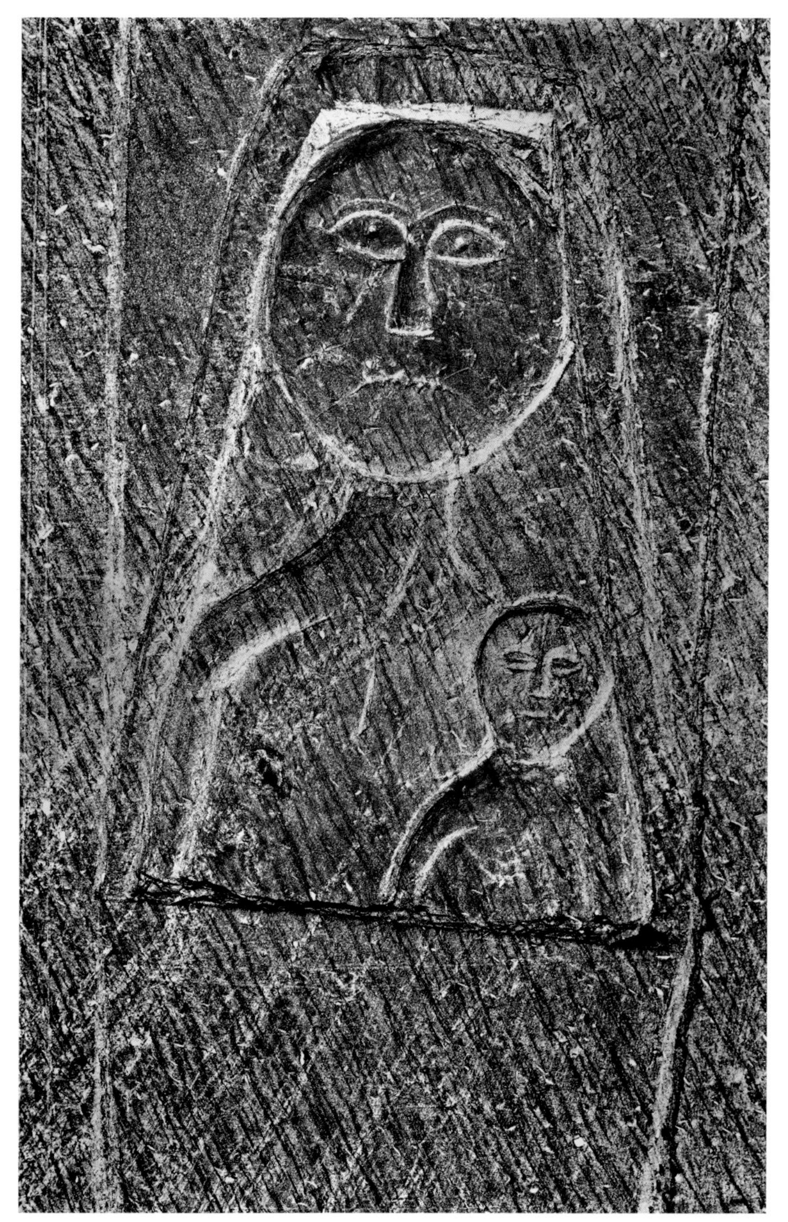

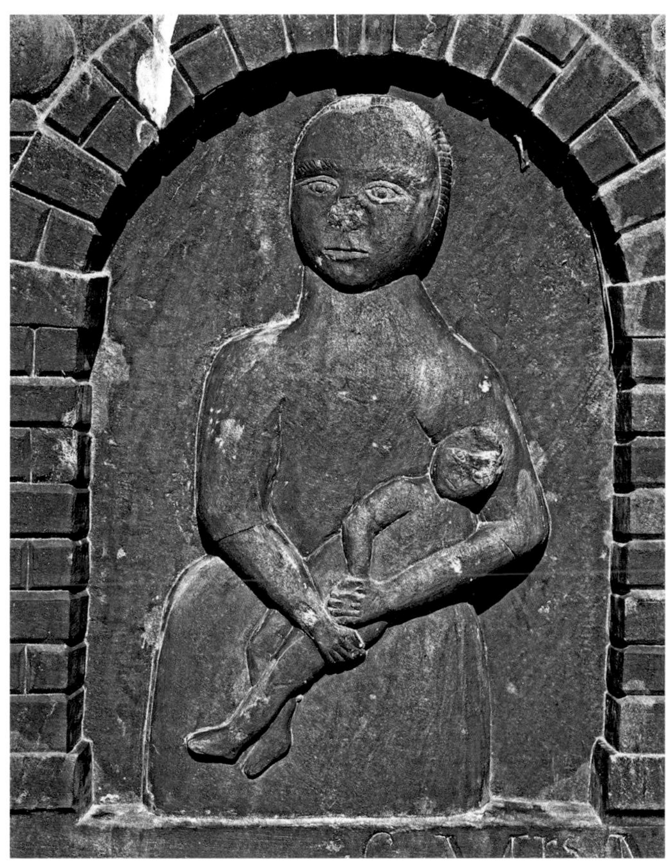

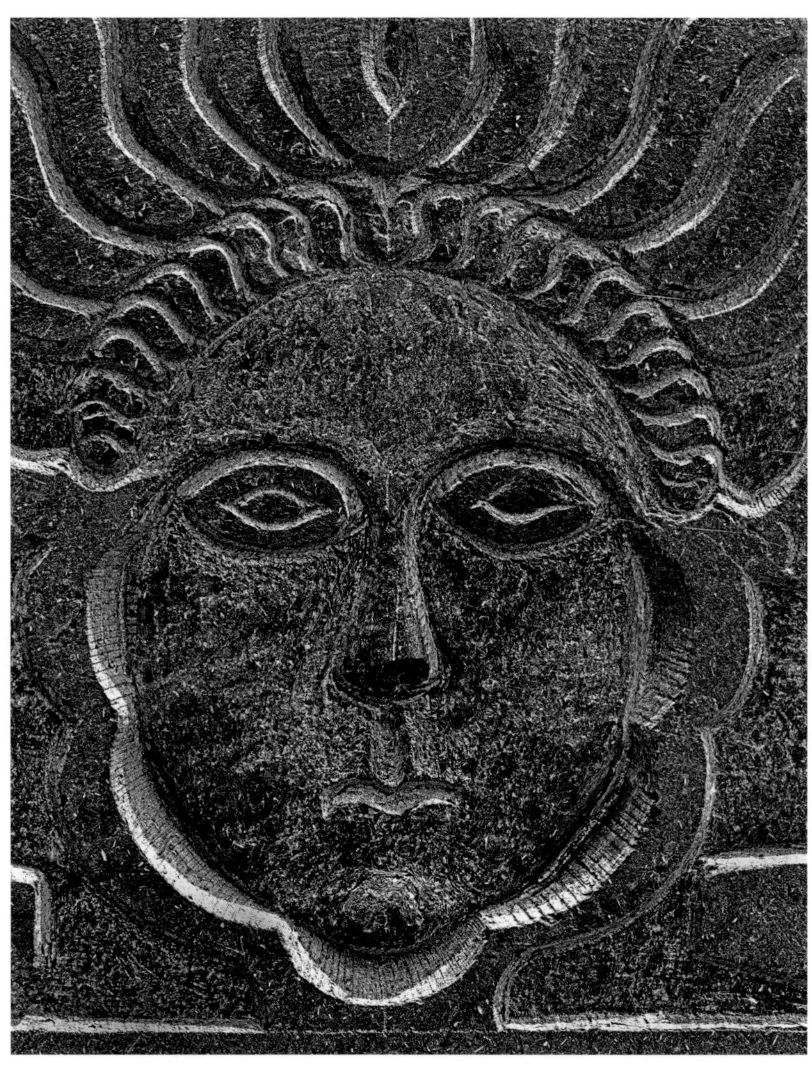

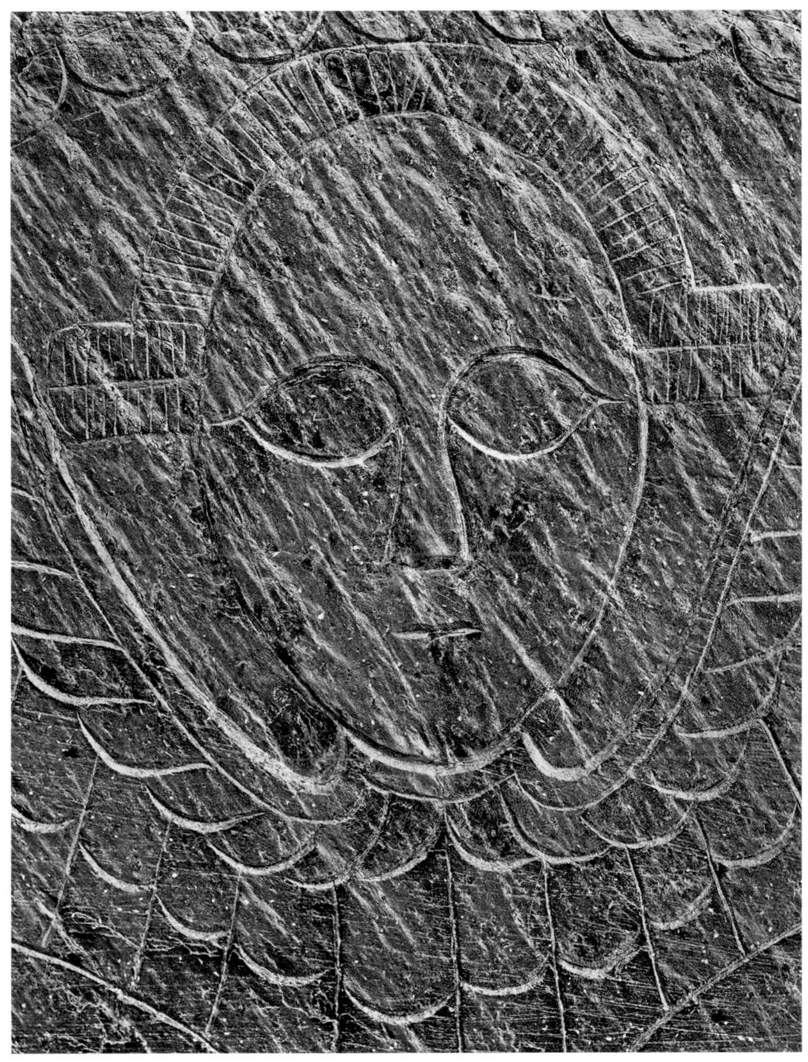

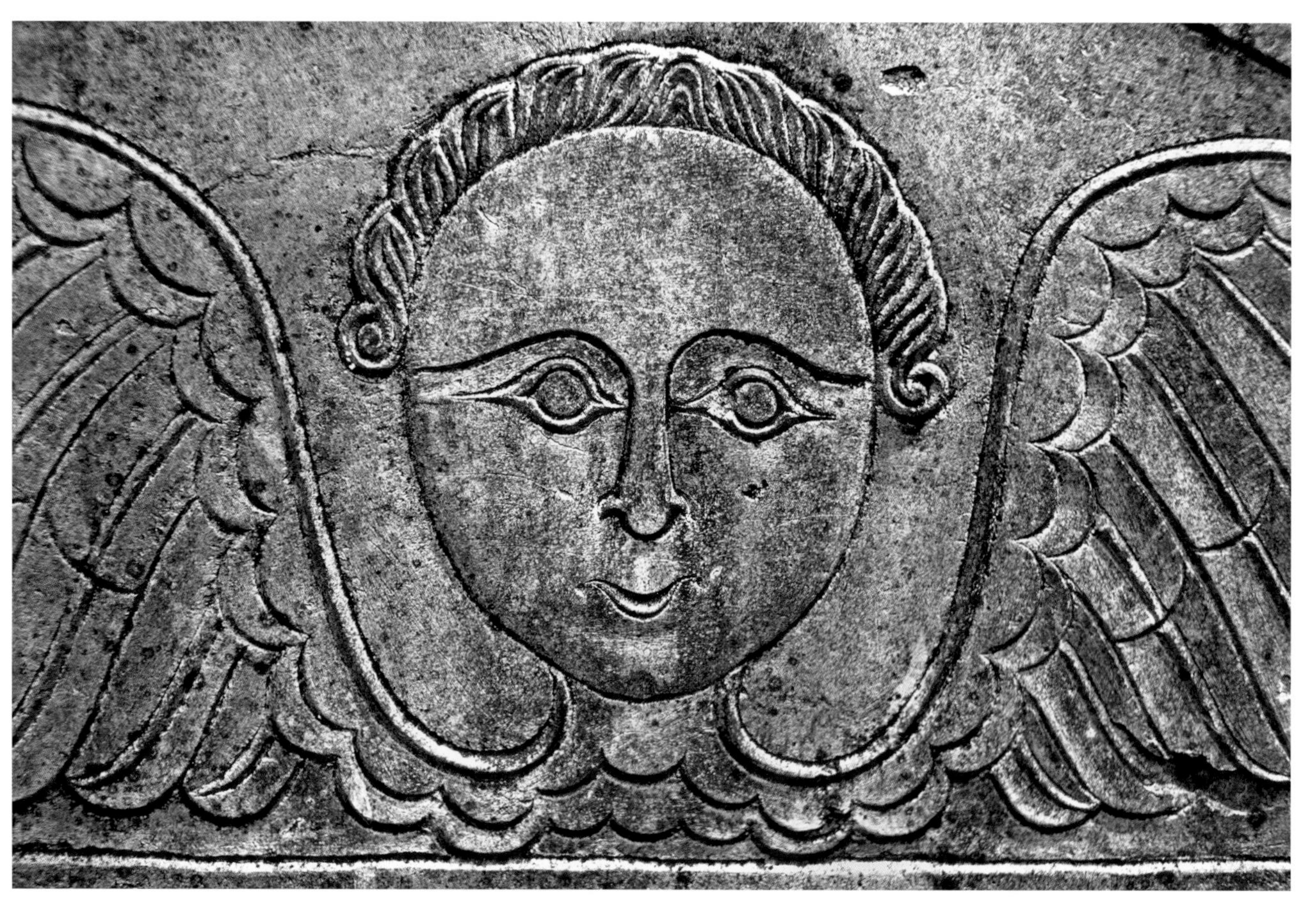

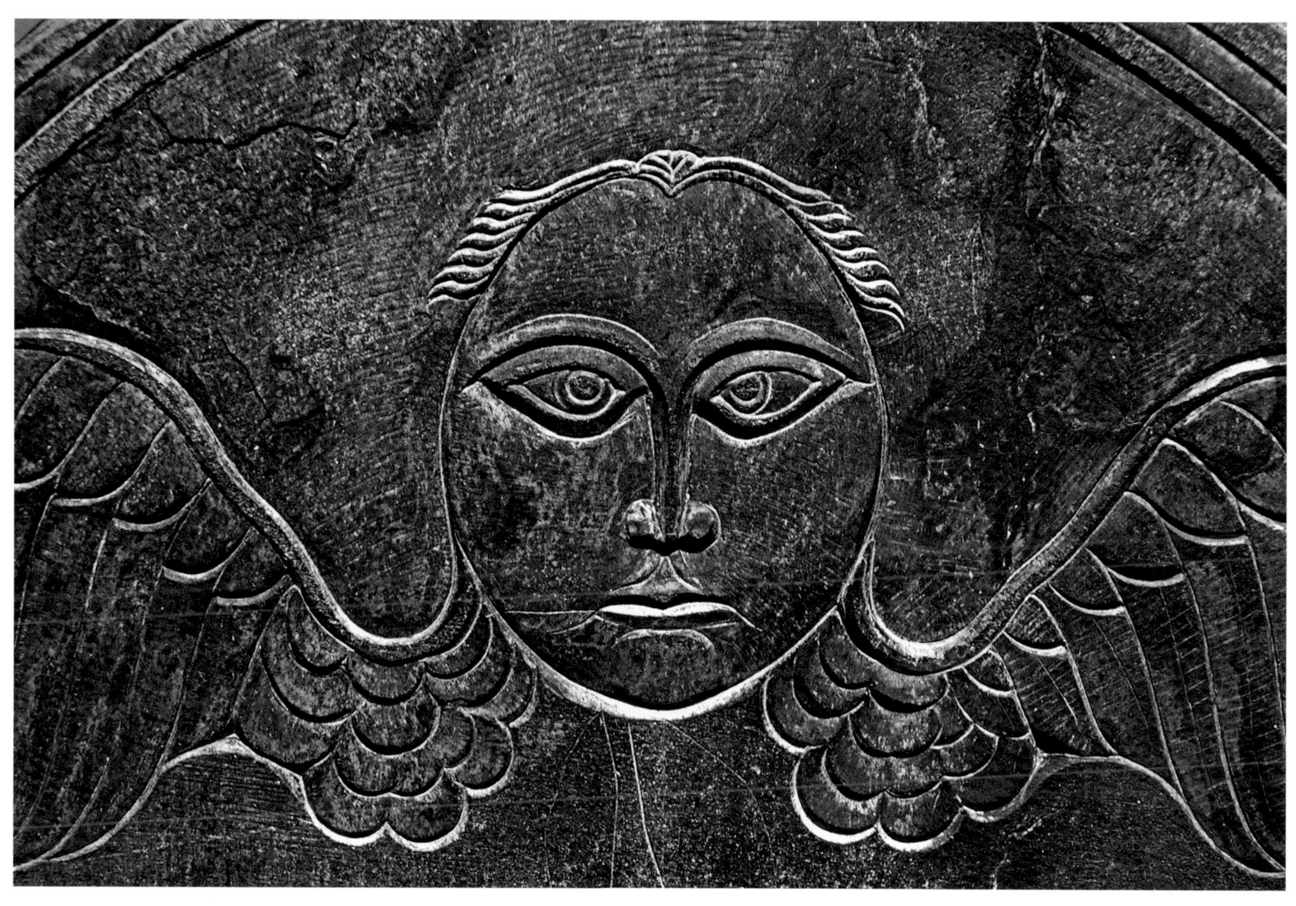

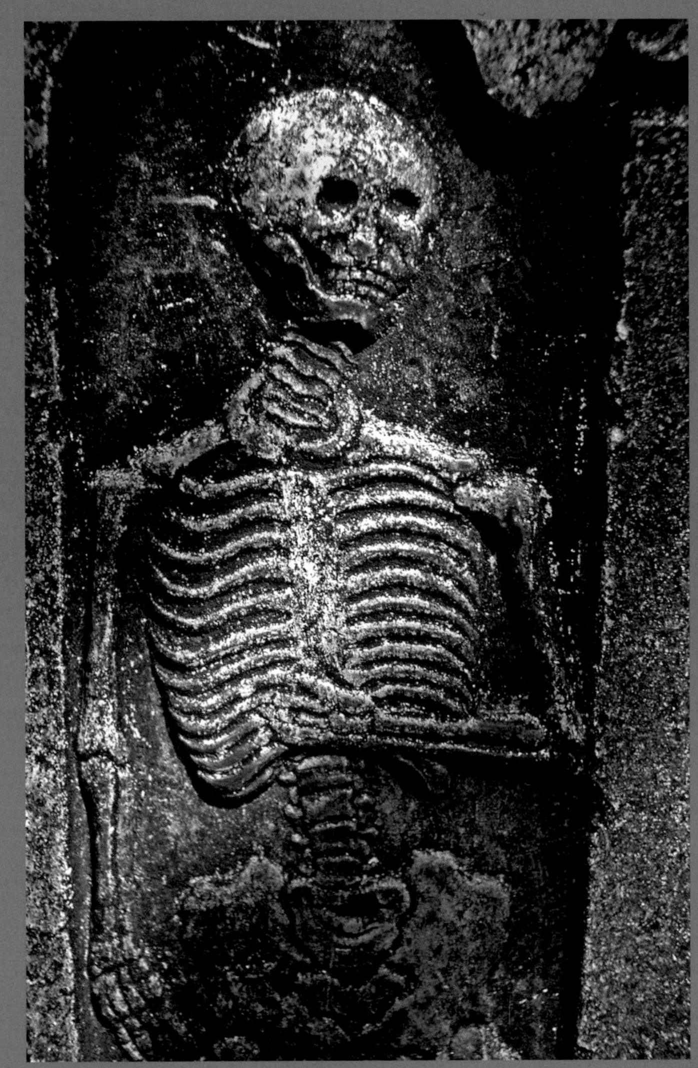

The God that holds you over the pit of hell, much in the same way as one holds a spider, or some loathsome insect, over the fire, abhors you and is dreadfully provoked; his wrath towards you burns like fire; he looks upon you as worthy of nothing else but to be cast into the fire; he is of purer eyes than to bear to have you in his sight; you are ten times more abominable in his eyes than the most hateful venomous serpent is in yours. You have offended him infinitely more than even a stubborn rebel did his prince; and yet, there is nothing but his hand that holds you from falling into the fire of every moment . . . yea, no other reason can be given why you do not this very moment drop down into hell.

Public address (1741), by Jonathan Edwards

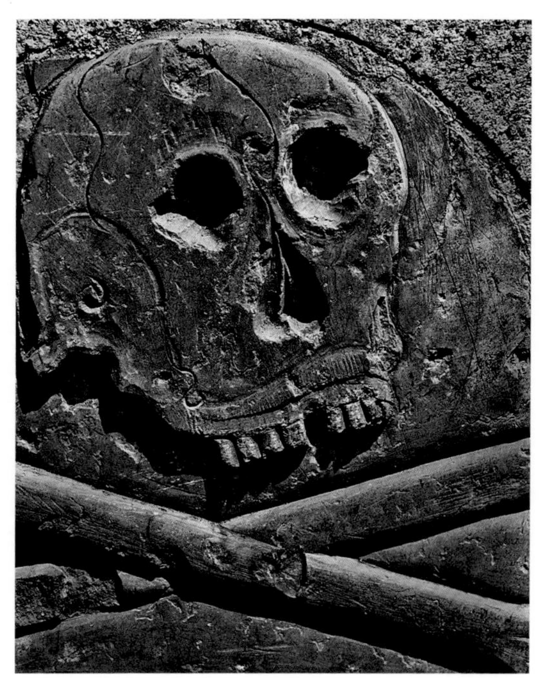

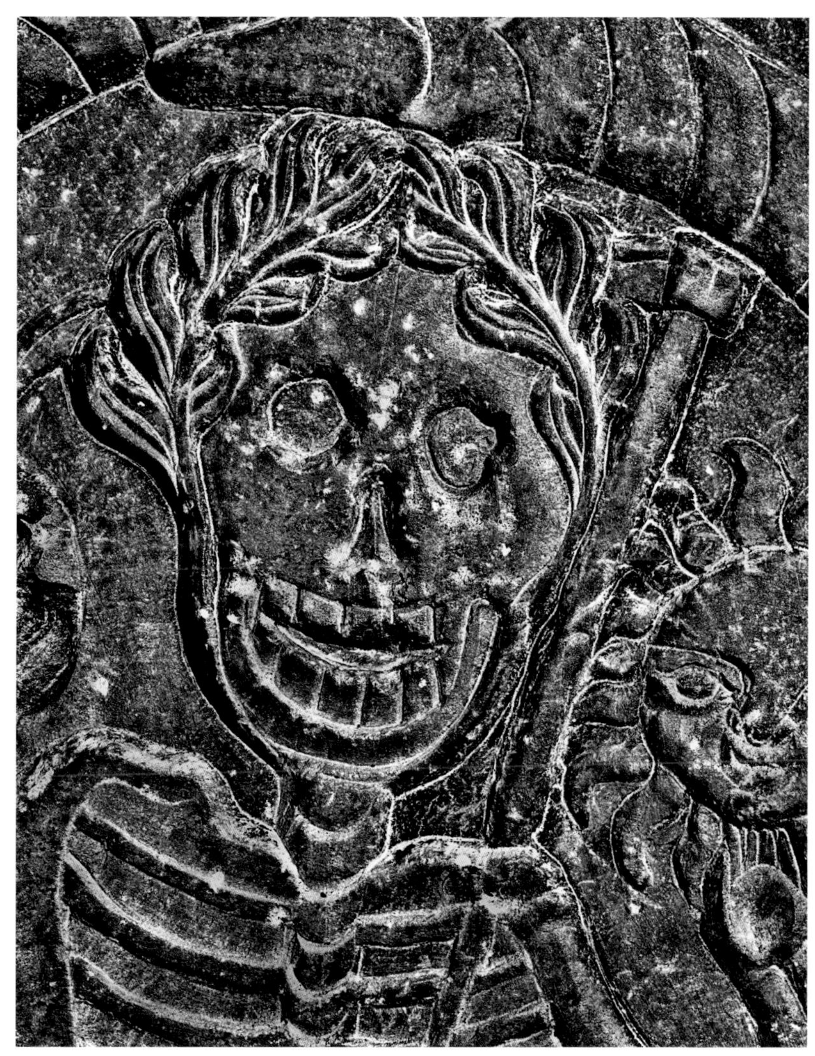

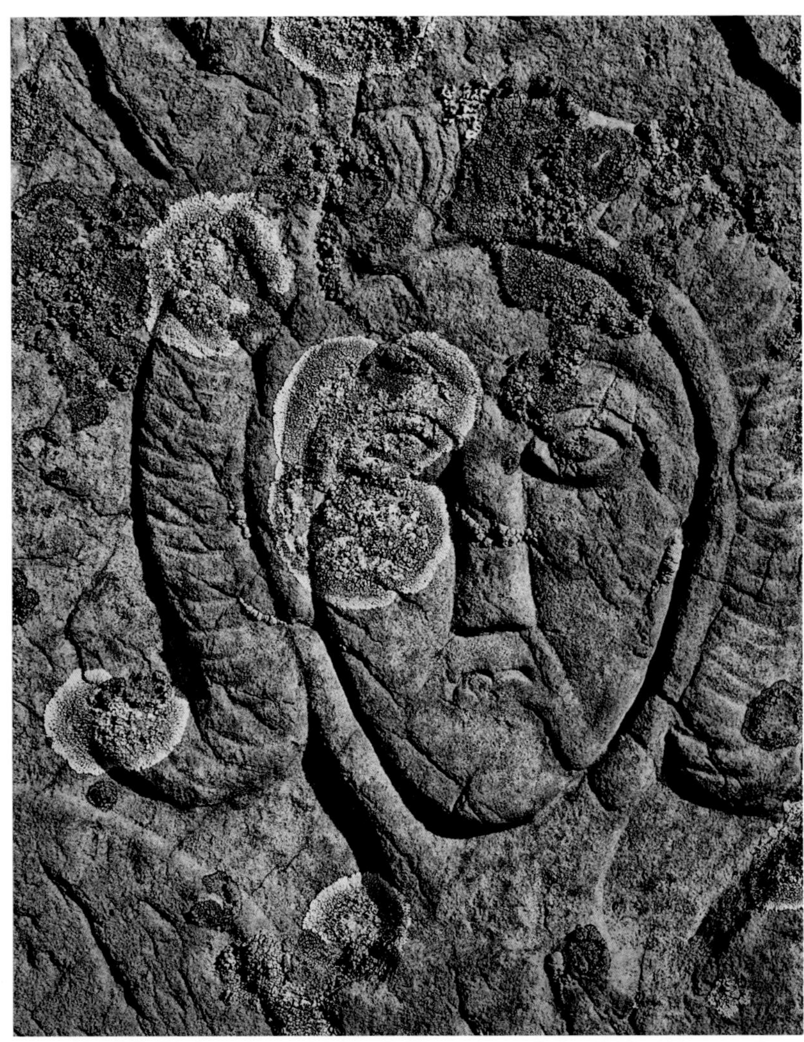

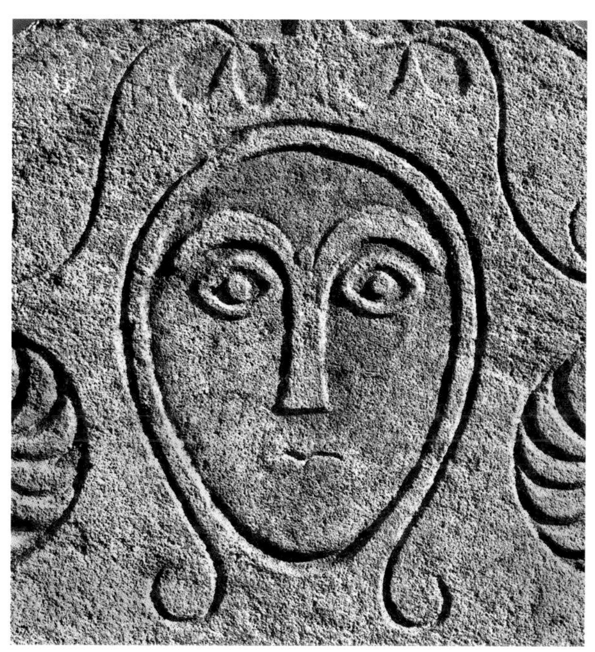

A company of vain, wicked men, having inflamed their blood in a tavern at Boston, and seeing that reverend, meek and holy minister of Christ Mr. Cotton, coming along the street, one of them tells his companions, "I'll go," saith he, "and put a trick on old Cotton."

Down he goes, and crossing his way, whispers these words into his ear: "Cotton," saith he, and "thou art an old fool."

Mr. Cotton replied, "I confess I am so; the Lord make both me and thee wiser, even wise unto salvation."

He relates this message to his wicked companions, which cast a great damp upon their sports, in the midst of a frolic.

Magnalia Christi Americana (1702)

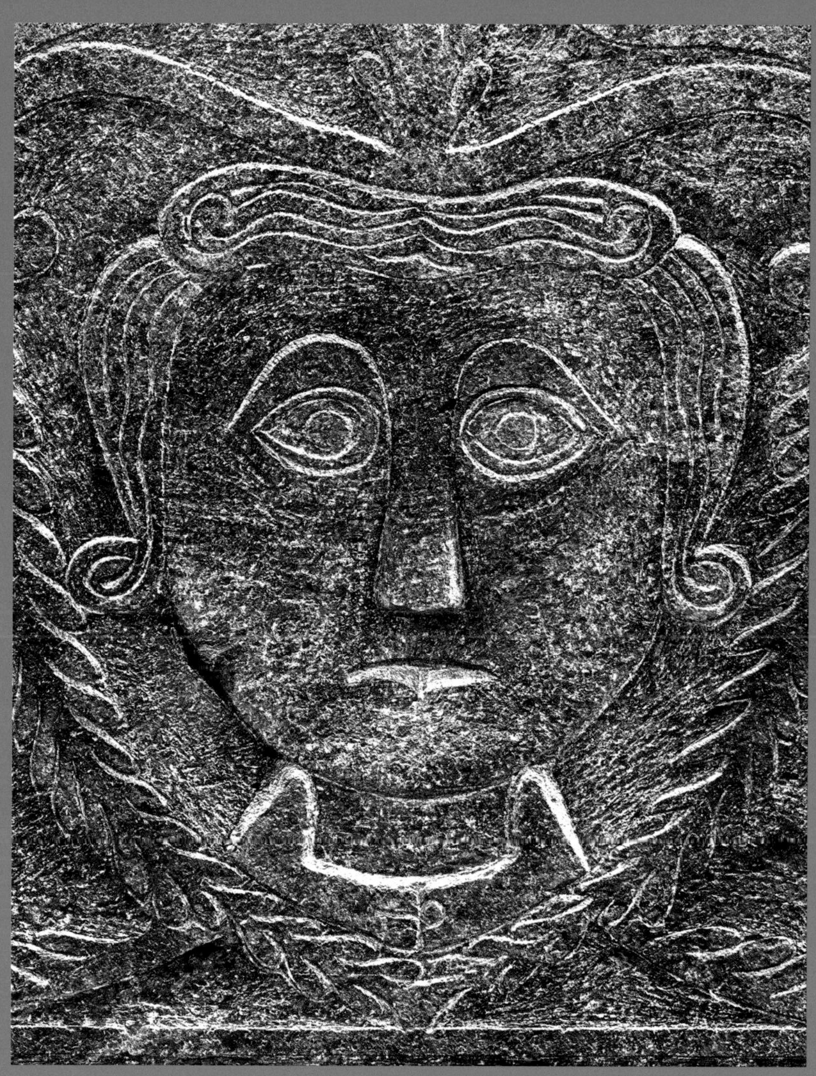

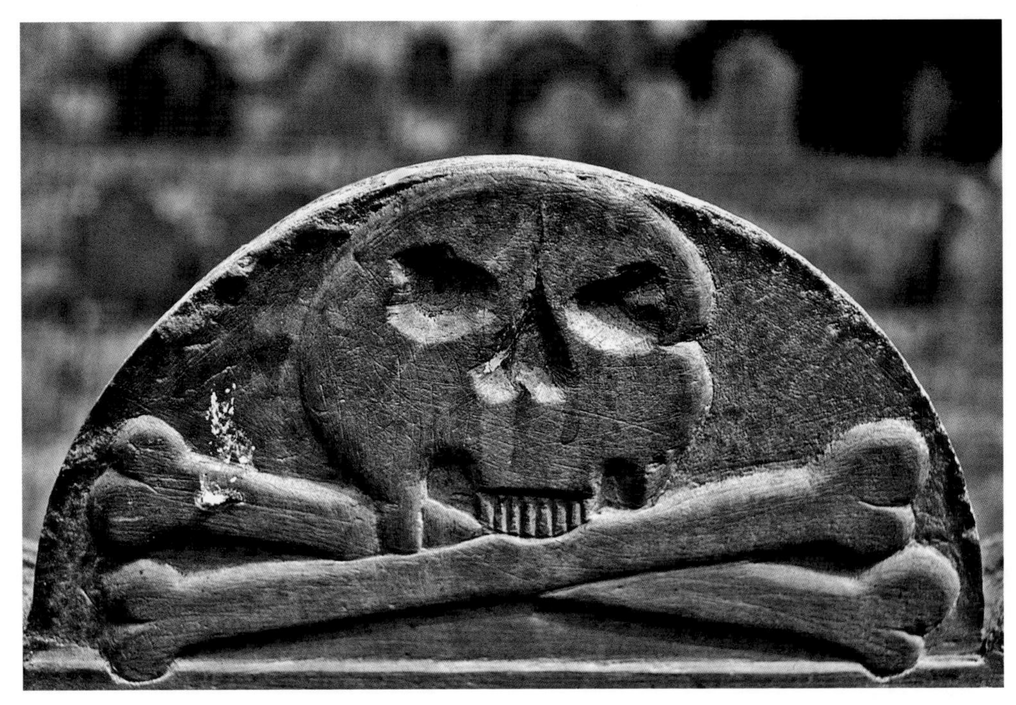

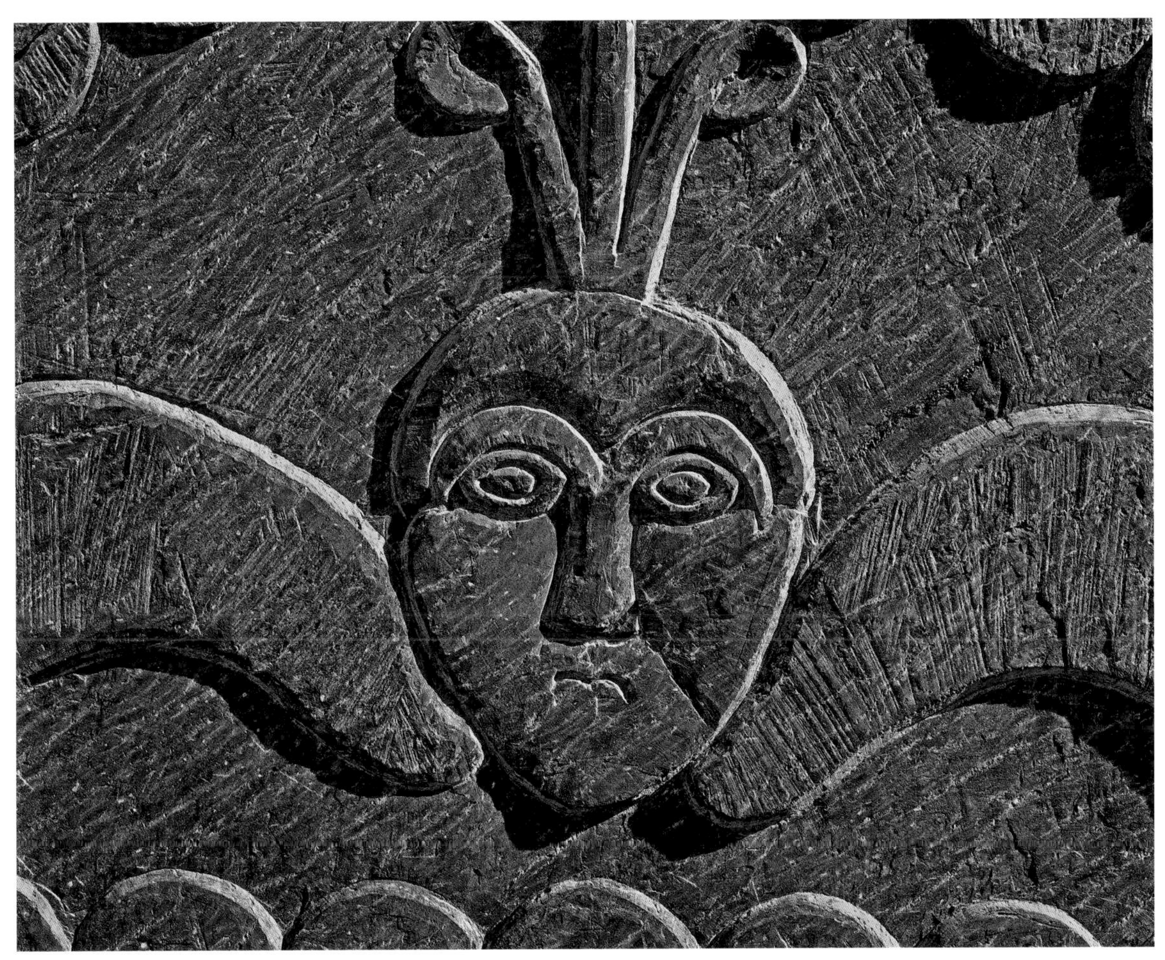

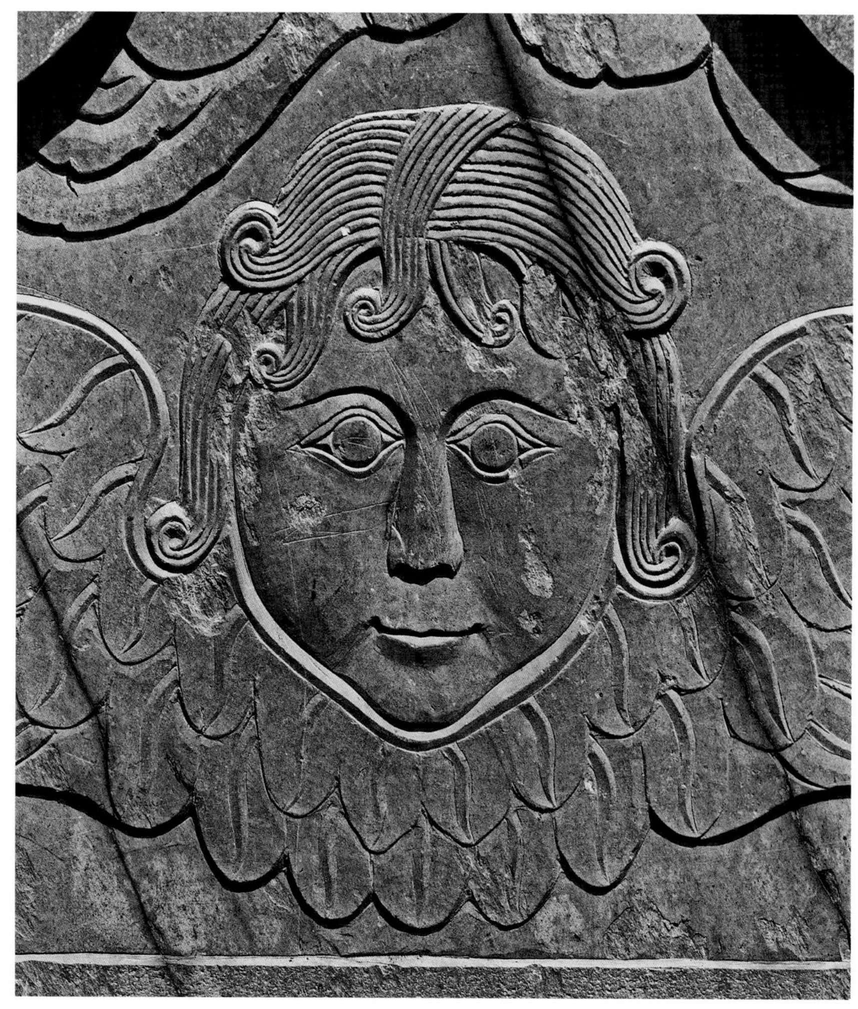

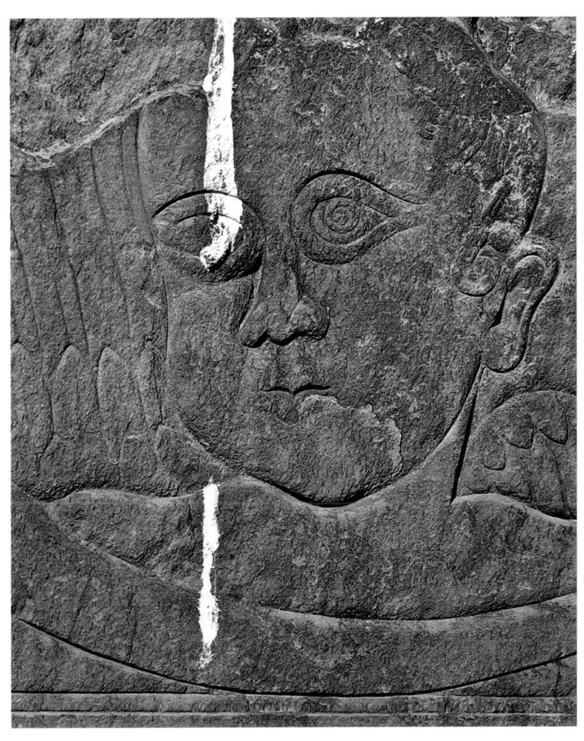

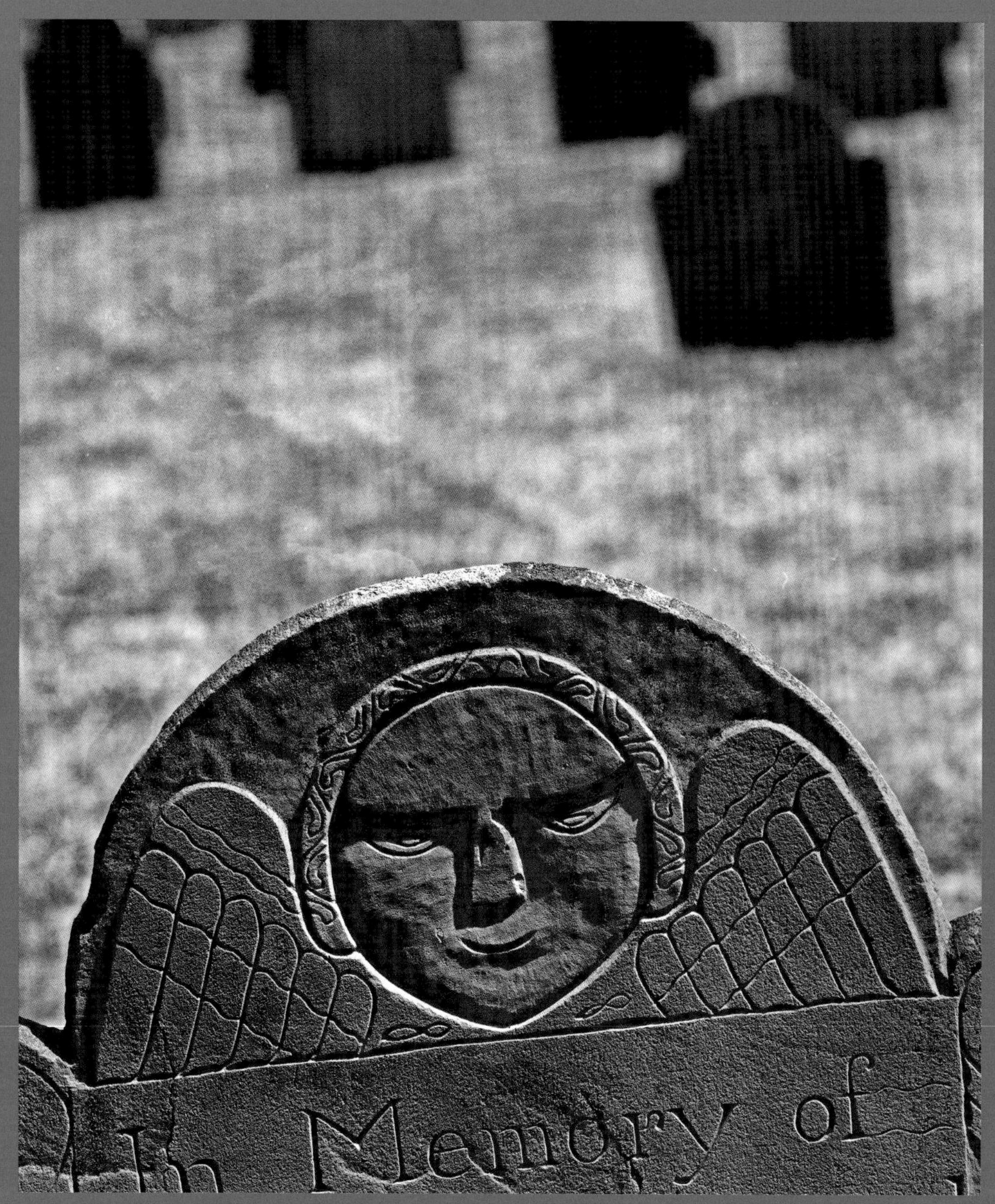
Memory of

An army of Devils is horribly broken in upon of the place which is the center, and after a sort, the first-born of our English settlements. And the houses of the good people there are filled with the doleful shrieks of their children and servants, tormented by invisible hands, with tortures altogether preternatural.

After the mischiefs there endeavored, and since in part conquered, the terrible plague of evil angels hath made its progress into some other places, where other persons in like manner have been diabolically handled. These our poor afflicted neighbors, quickly after they became infected and infested with these demons, arrive to a capacity of discerning the shapes of their troublers. And notwithstanding the great and just suspicion that the demon might impose the shapes of innocent persons in their spectral exhibition upon the sufferers (which may prove no small part of the witch-plot), yet many of the persons thus represented, being examined, have been convicted of a very damnable witchcraft. Yea, more than twenty have confessed that they have signed unto a book which the Devil showed them, and engaged in his hellish design of bewitching and ruining our land.

The Wonders of the Invisible World (1692), by Cotton Mather

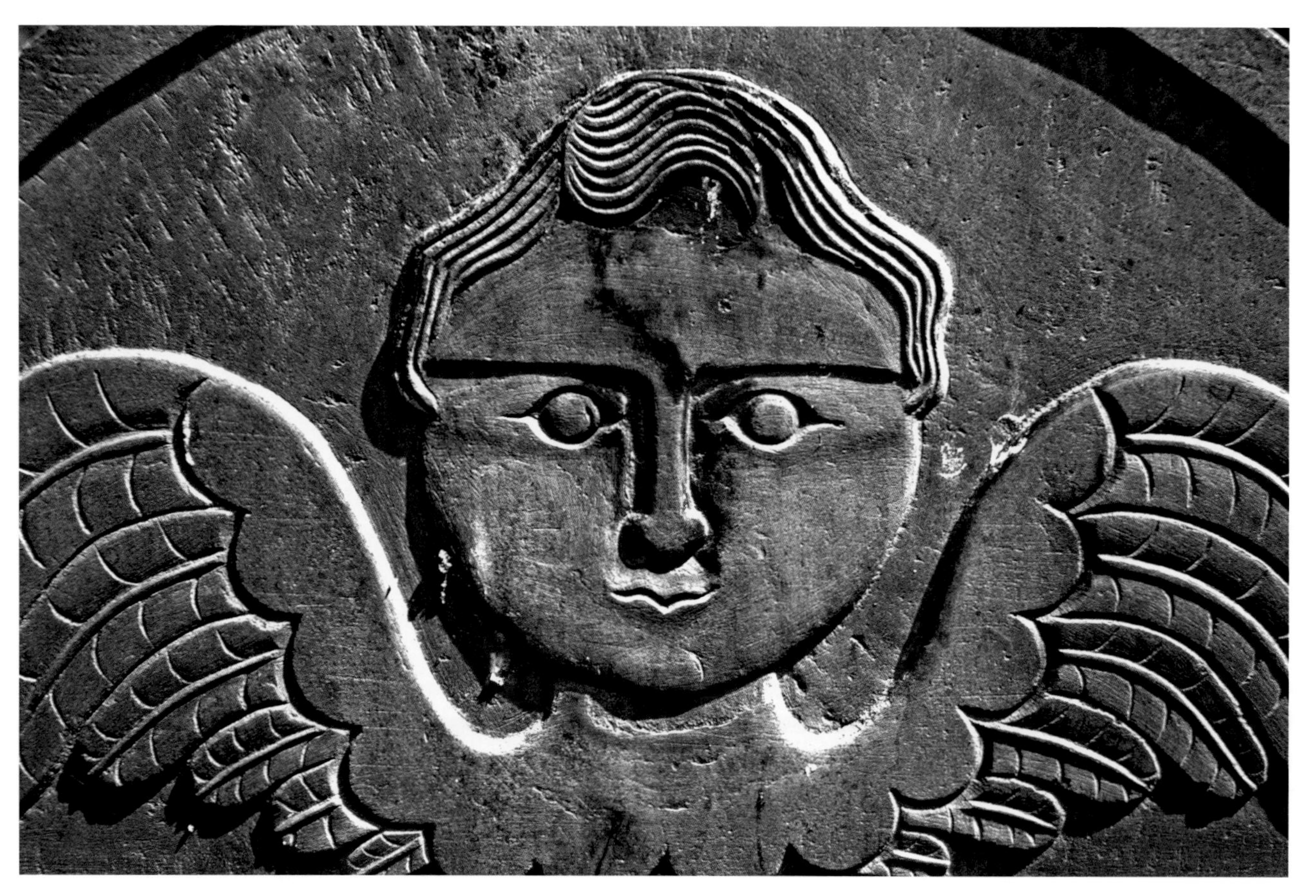

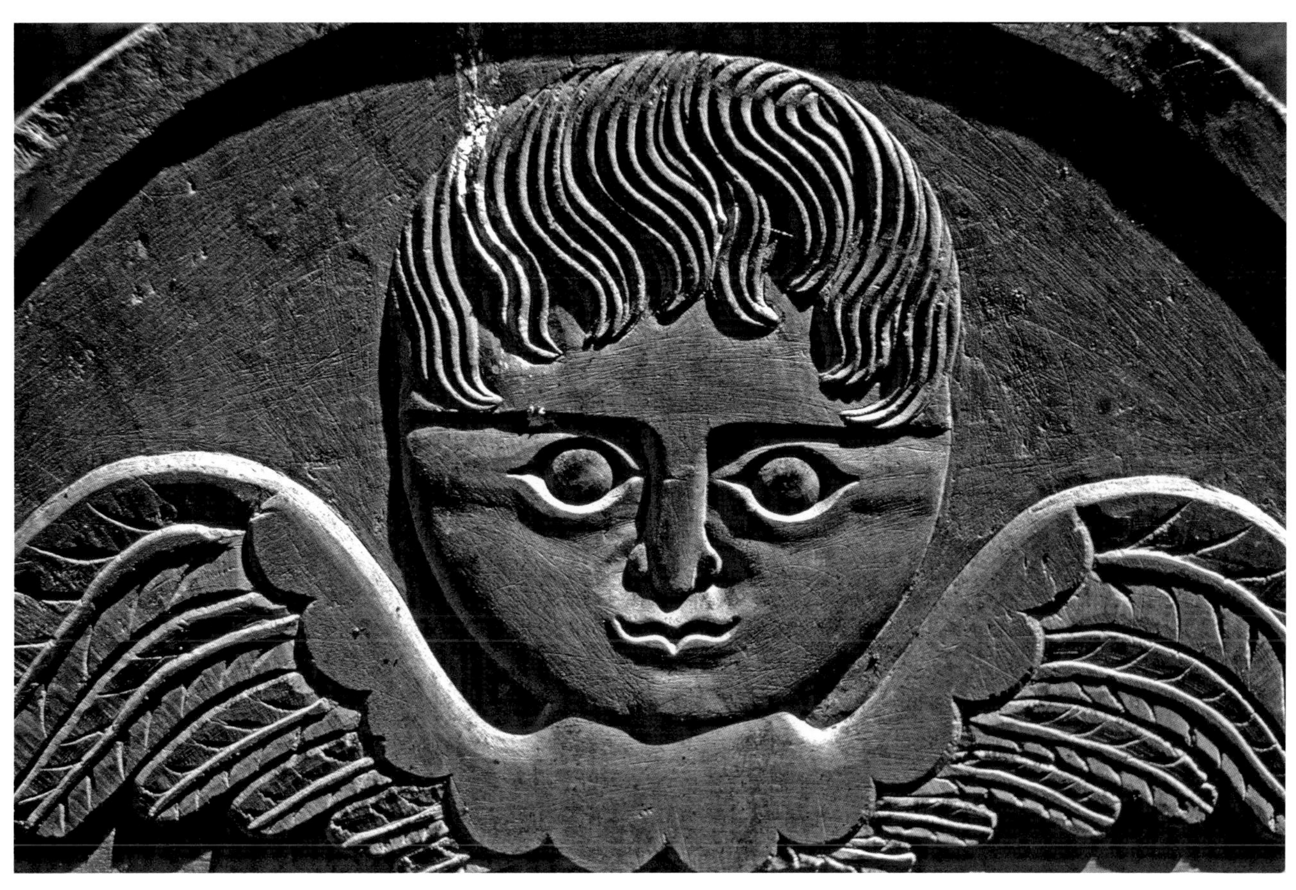

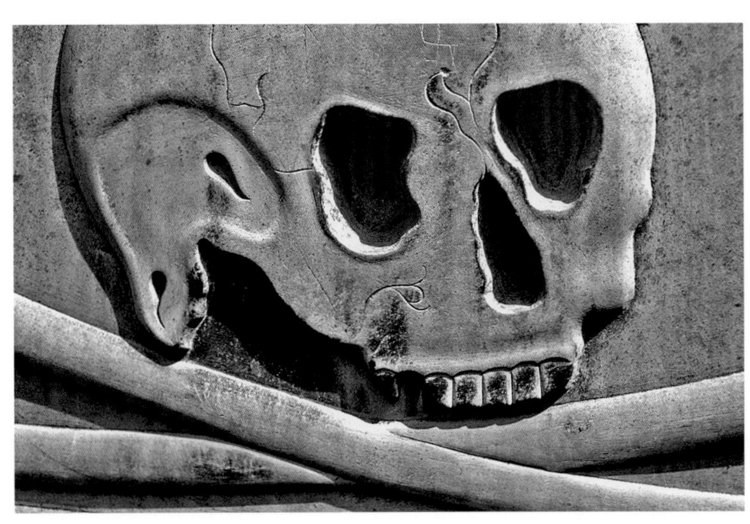

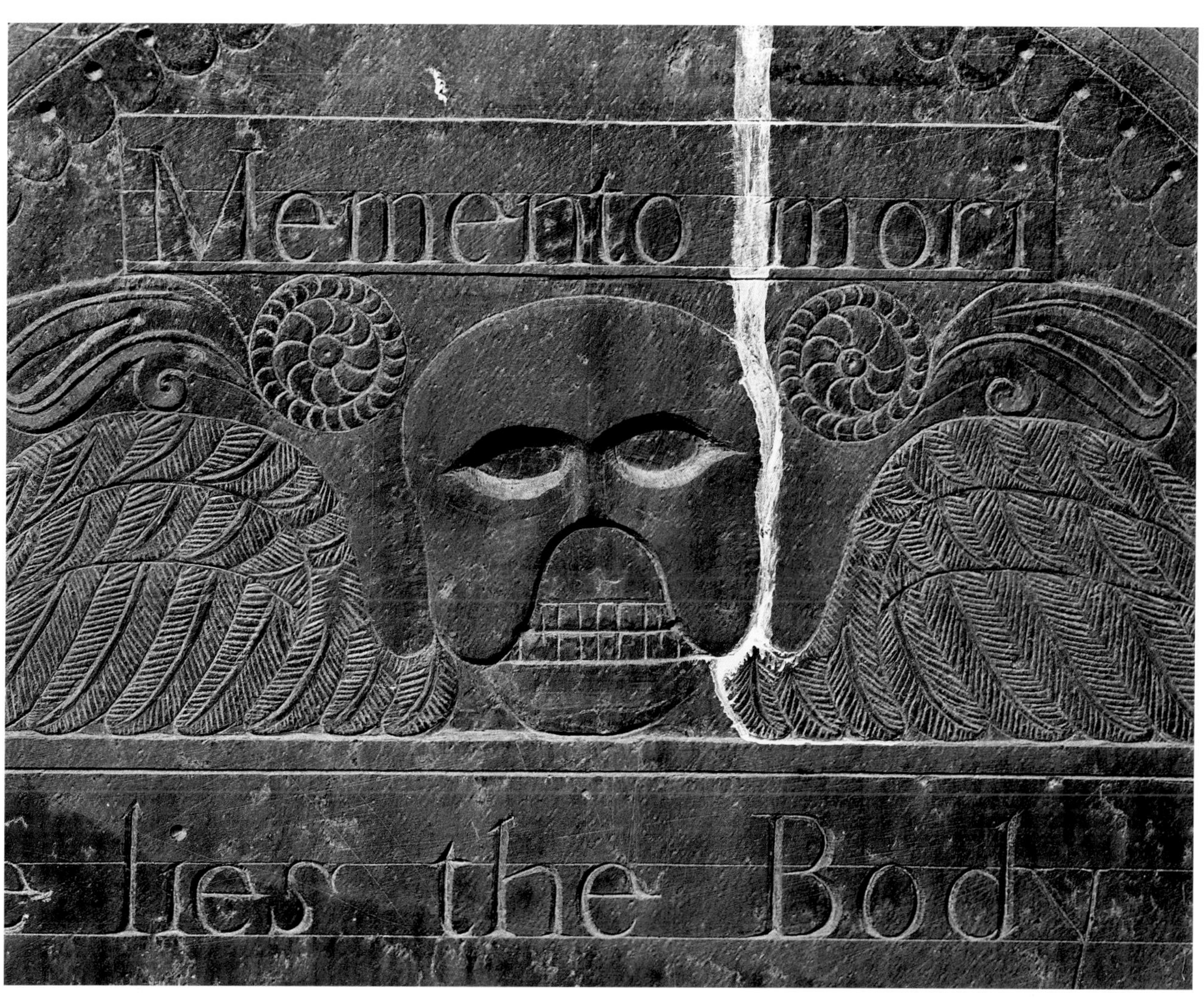
Memento mori
lies the Body

DECEMBER 22 [1727].

The day after the fast, was interred. . . . I was inclined before, and having a pair of gloves sent me, I determined to go to the funeral if the weather proved favorable, which it did; and I hired Blake's coach with four horses. My son, Mr. Cooper and Mr. Prince went with me. Refreshed there with meat and drink; got thither about half an hour past one. It was sad to see [death] triumphed over my dear friend! I rode in my coach to the burying place, not being able to get nearer by reason of the many horses. From thence went directly up the hill where the smith's shop, and so home very comfortably and easily, the ground being mollified. But when I came to my own gate, going in, I fell down, a board slipping under my left foot, my right leg raised off the skin and put me to a great deal of pain, especially when 'twas washed with rum. It was good for me that I was thus afflicted, that my spirit might be brought into a frame more suitable to the solemnity, which is apt to be too light. And by the loss of some of my skin and blood, I might be awakened to prepare for my own dissolution.

Diary of Samuel Sewall

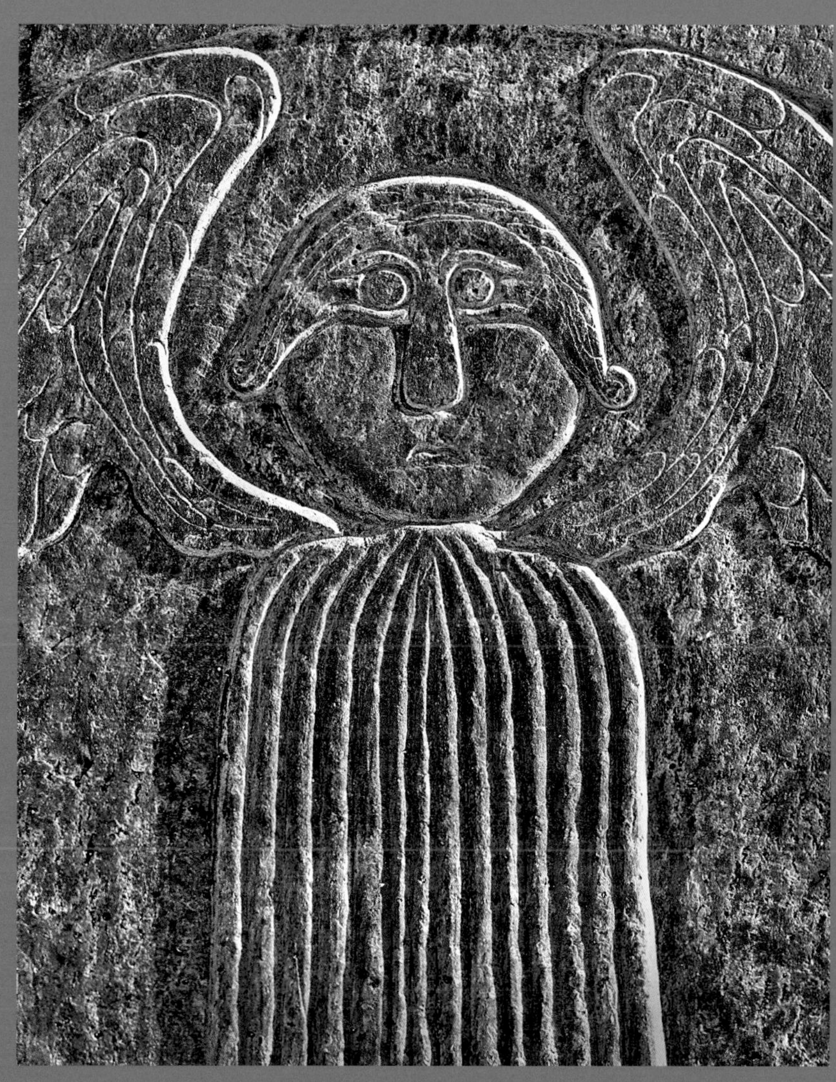

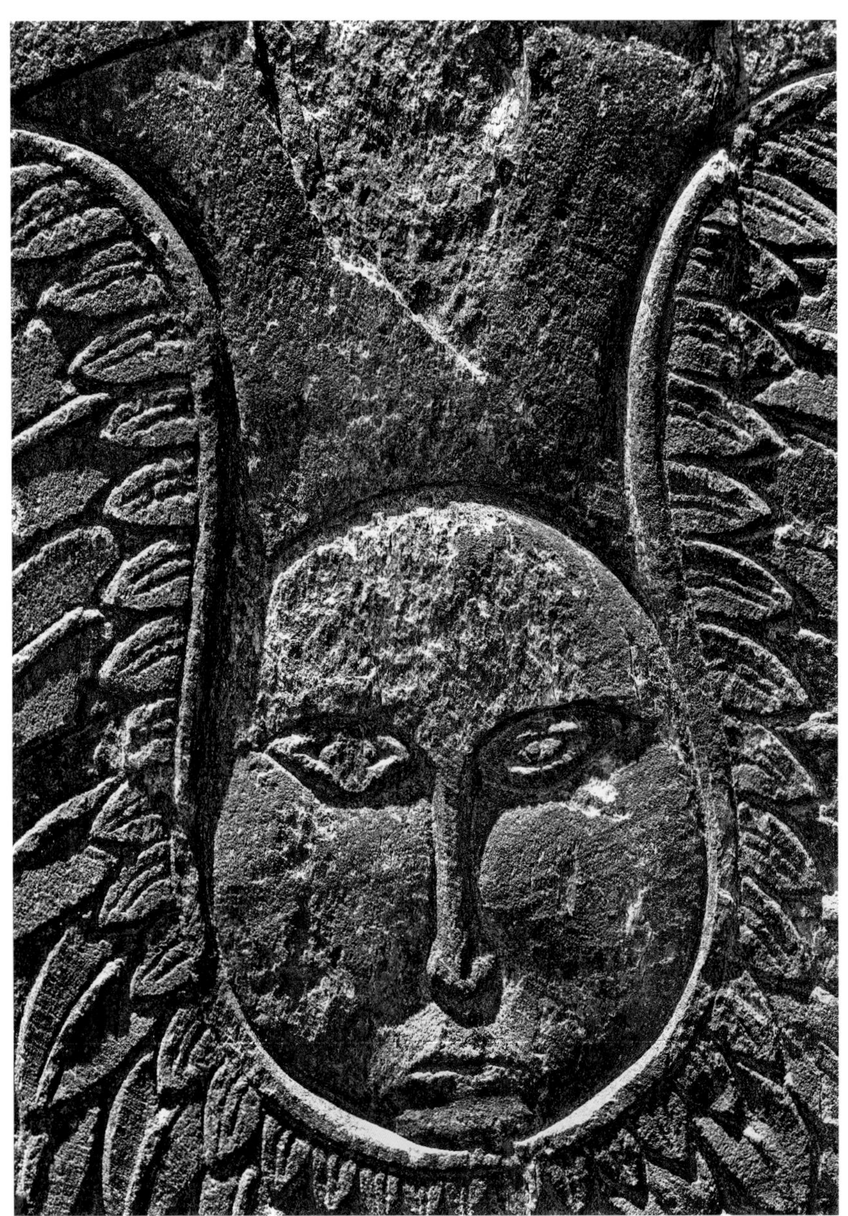

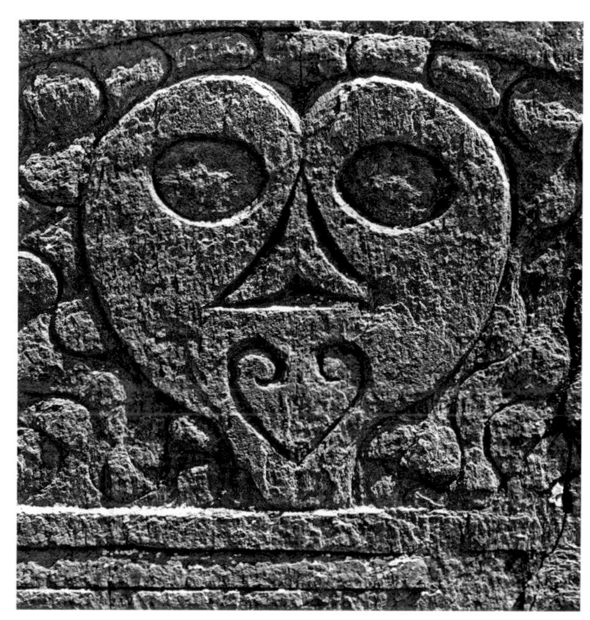

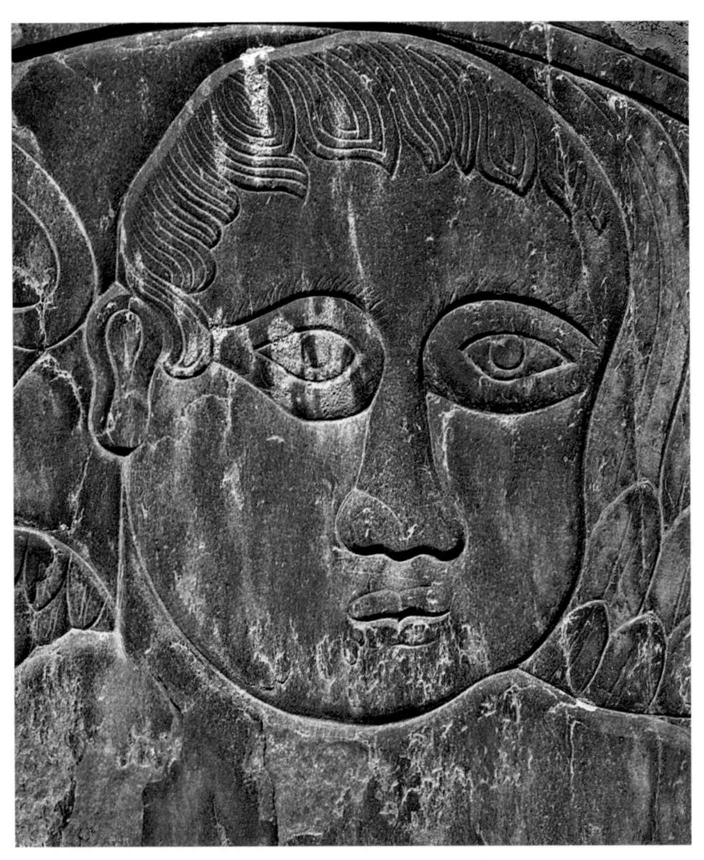

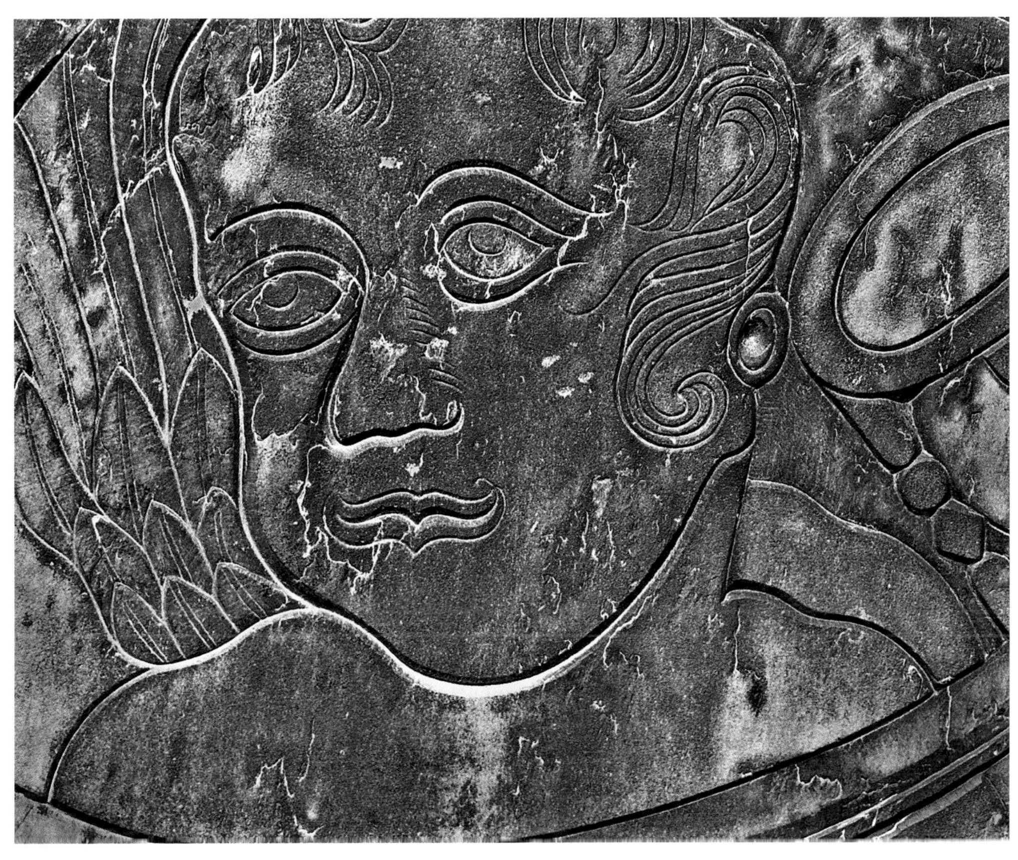

Within this tomb a patriot lies
That was both pious, just, and wise,
To truth a shield, to right a wall,
To sectaries a whip and maul,
A magazine of history,
A prizer of good company,
In manners pleasant and severe;
The good him loved, the bad did fear.
And when his time with years was spent,
If some rejoiced, more did lament.

"Epitaph on a Patriot," by Anne Bradstreet

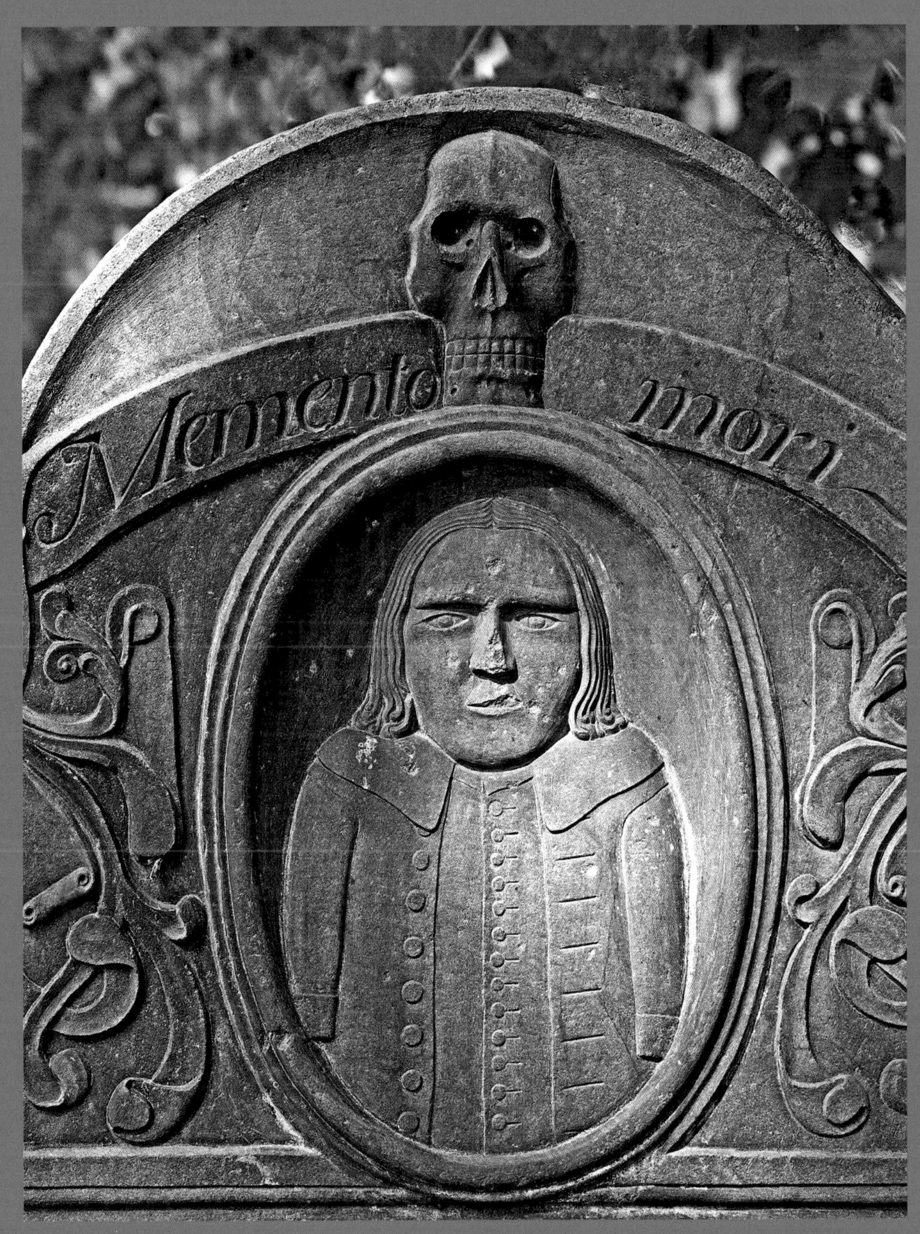
Memento mori

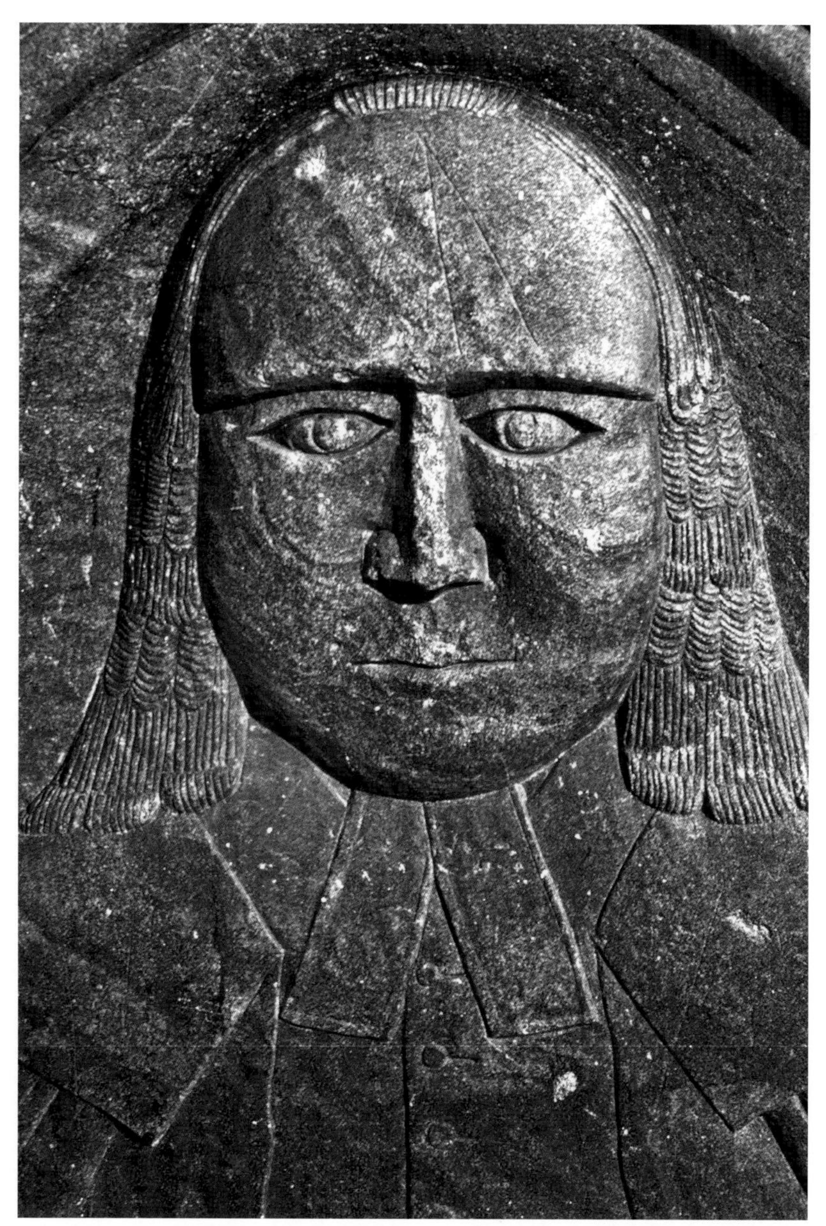

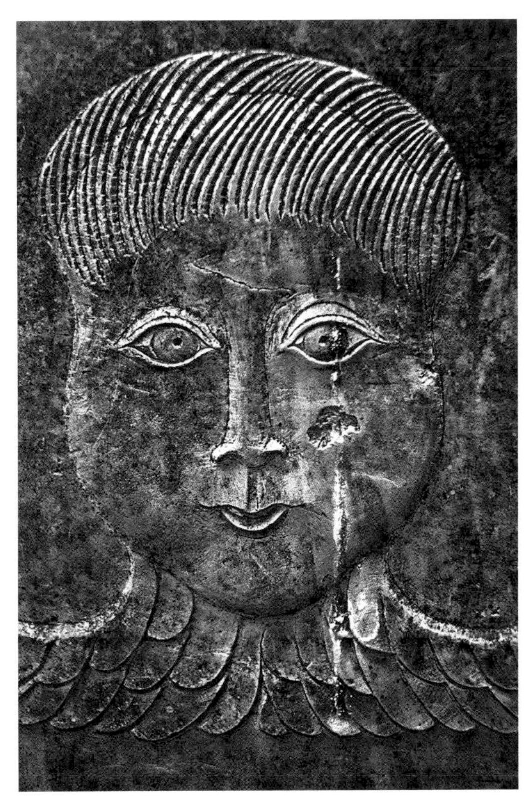

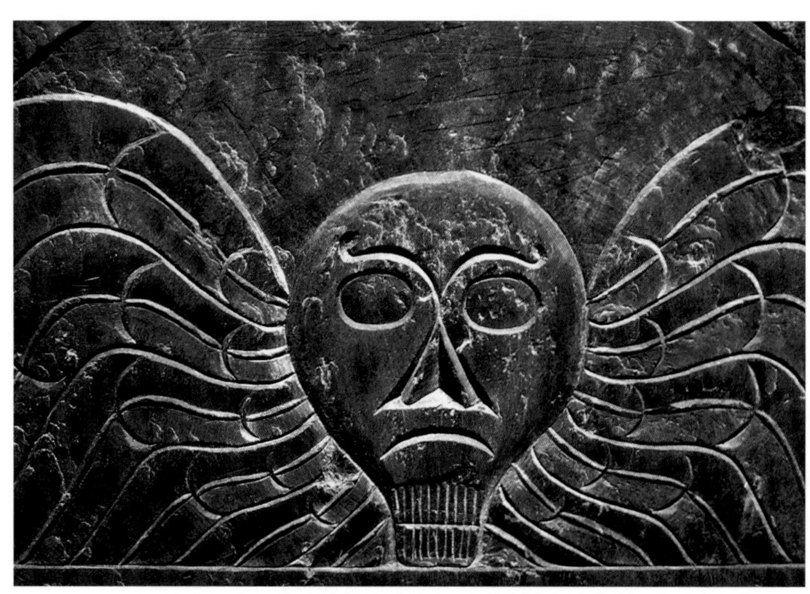

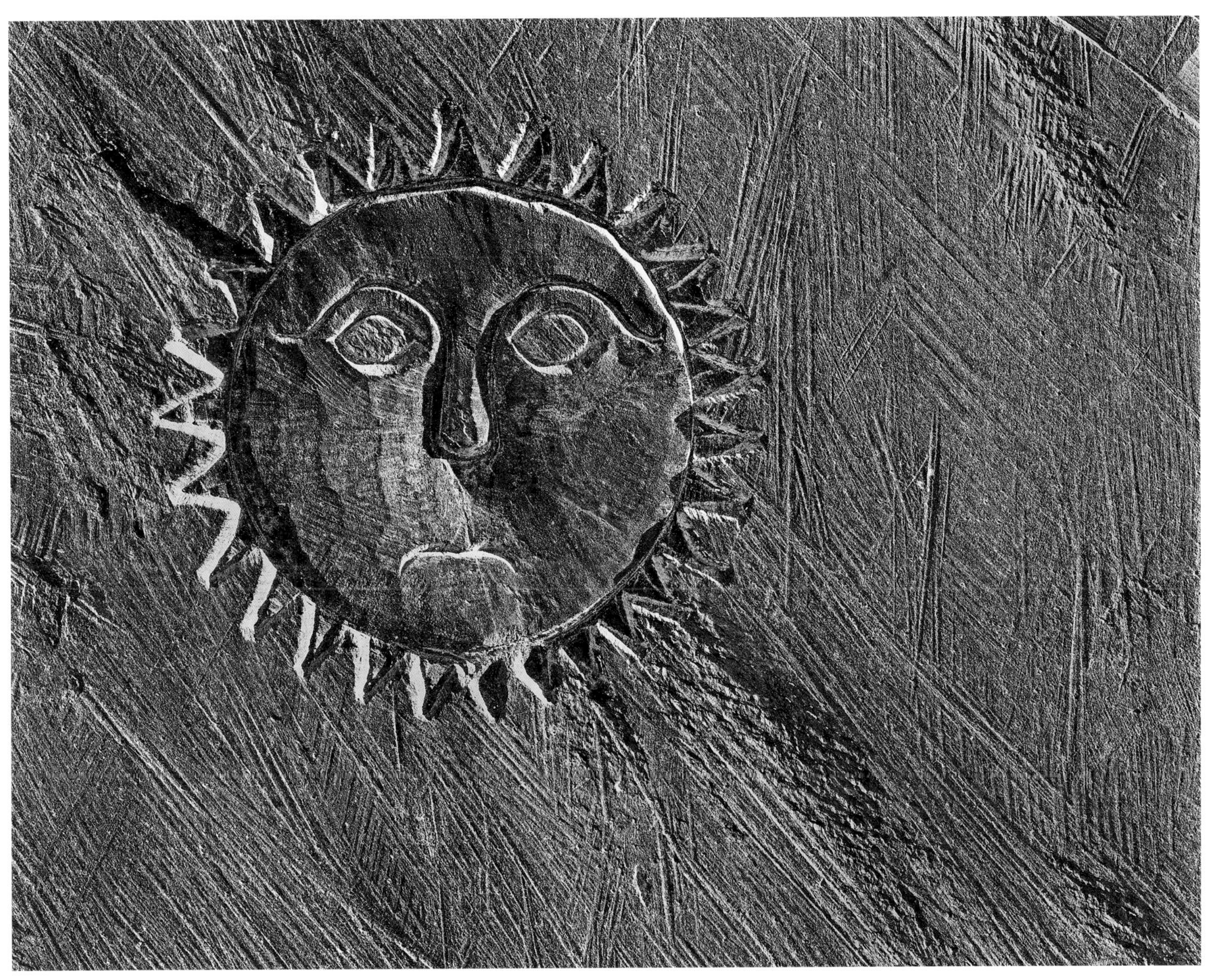

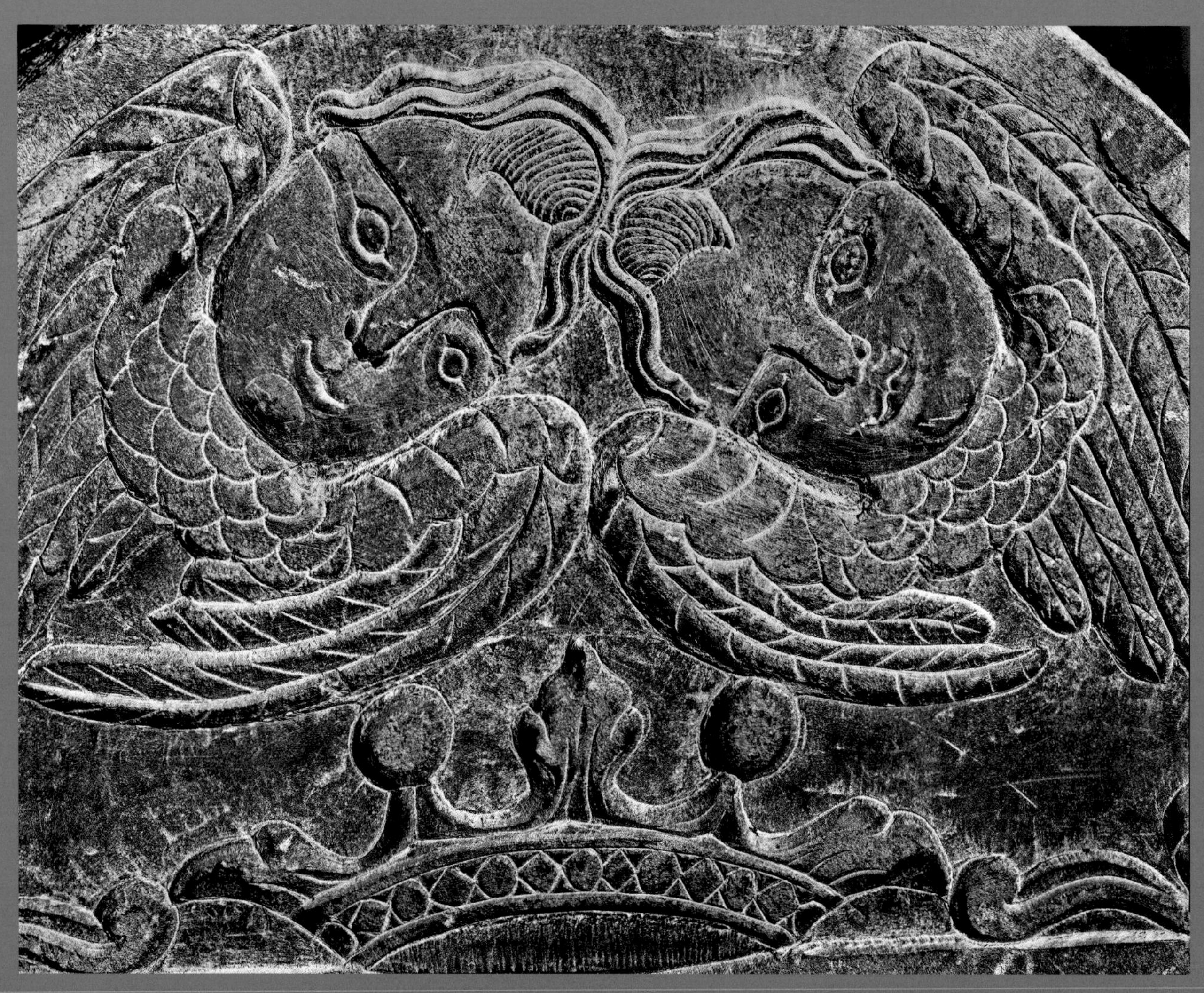

His bodily pains continued upon him until April 22, when in the morning his son aforementioned, coming to visit him, asked his father if he knew him; to whom he replied that he did, but was not able to speak any more to him. Whereupon his son saying, "Now you will speedily be in the joy of your Lord," his father lifted up his hands, but could not speak. Not long after, his son again spoke to him, saying, "You will quickly see Jesus Christ, and that will make amends for all your pains and sorrows." At which words, his father again lifted up his hands; but after that he took notice of no person or thing, but continuing speechless until 10 p.m., he quietly breathed forth his last. Thus did that light, that had been shining in the church above fifty years, expire.

The Life and Death of That Revered Man in God, Mr. Richard Mather,
by Increase Mather whose father was Richard Increase Mather

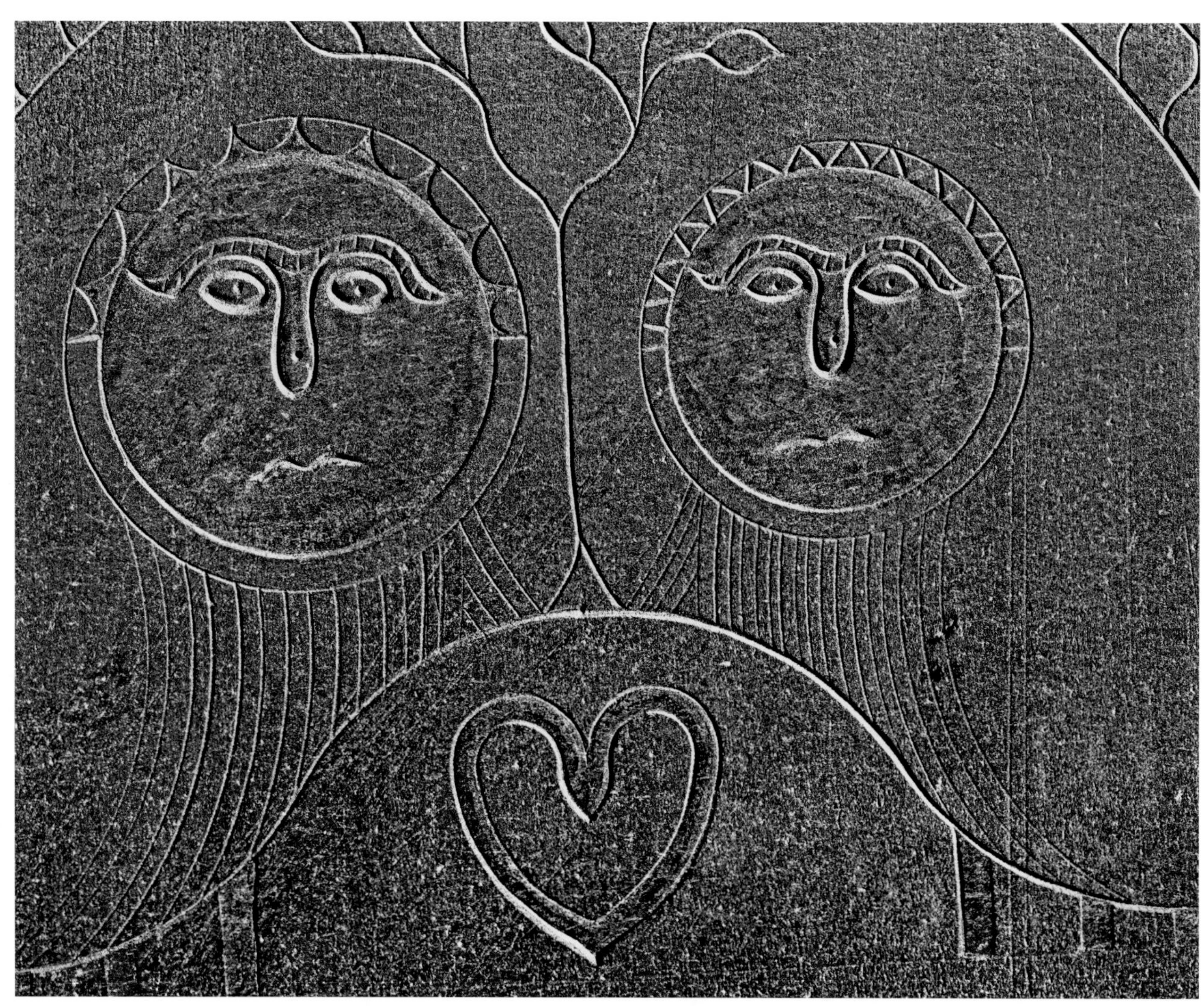

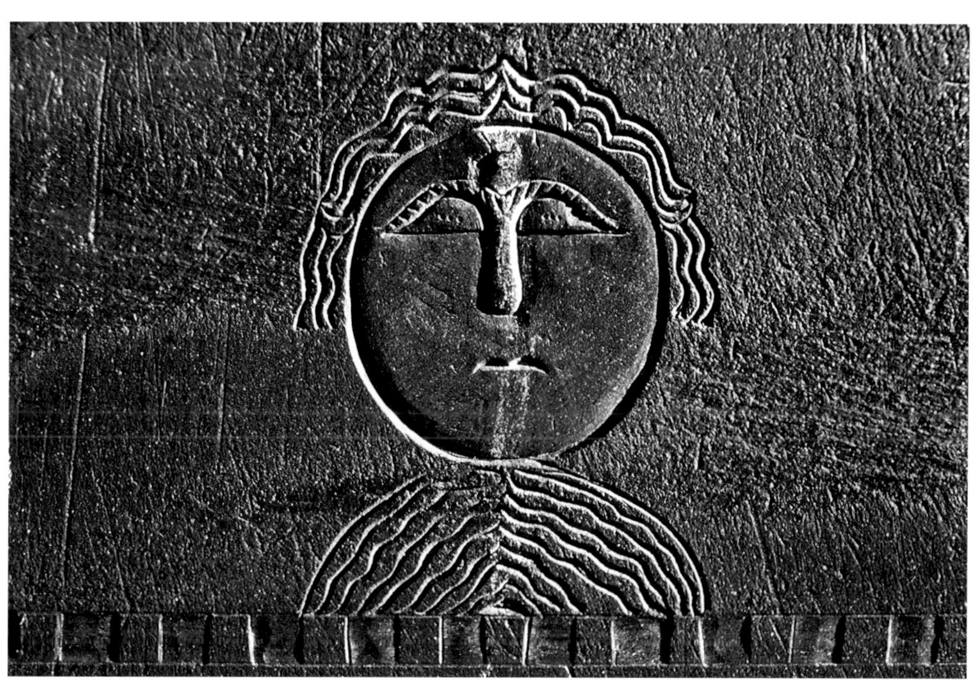

[APRIL 13, 1641.]

A godly woman of the church of Boston, dwelling sometimes in London, brought with her a parcel of very fine linen of great value, which she set her heart too much upon, and had been at charge to have it all newly washed, and curiously folded and pressed, and so left it in press in her parlor overnight. She had a Negro maid went into the room very late, and let fall some snuff of the candle upon the linen, so as by the morning all the linen was burned to tinder, and the boards underneath, and some stools and a part of the wainscot burned, and never perceived by any in the house, though some lodged in the chamber overhead, and no ceiling between. But it pleased God that the loss of this linen did her much good, both in taking off her heart from worldly comforts, and in preparing her for a far greater affliction by the untimely death of her husband, who was slain not long after at Isle of Providence.

Journal by John Winthrop

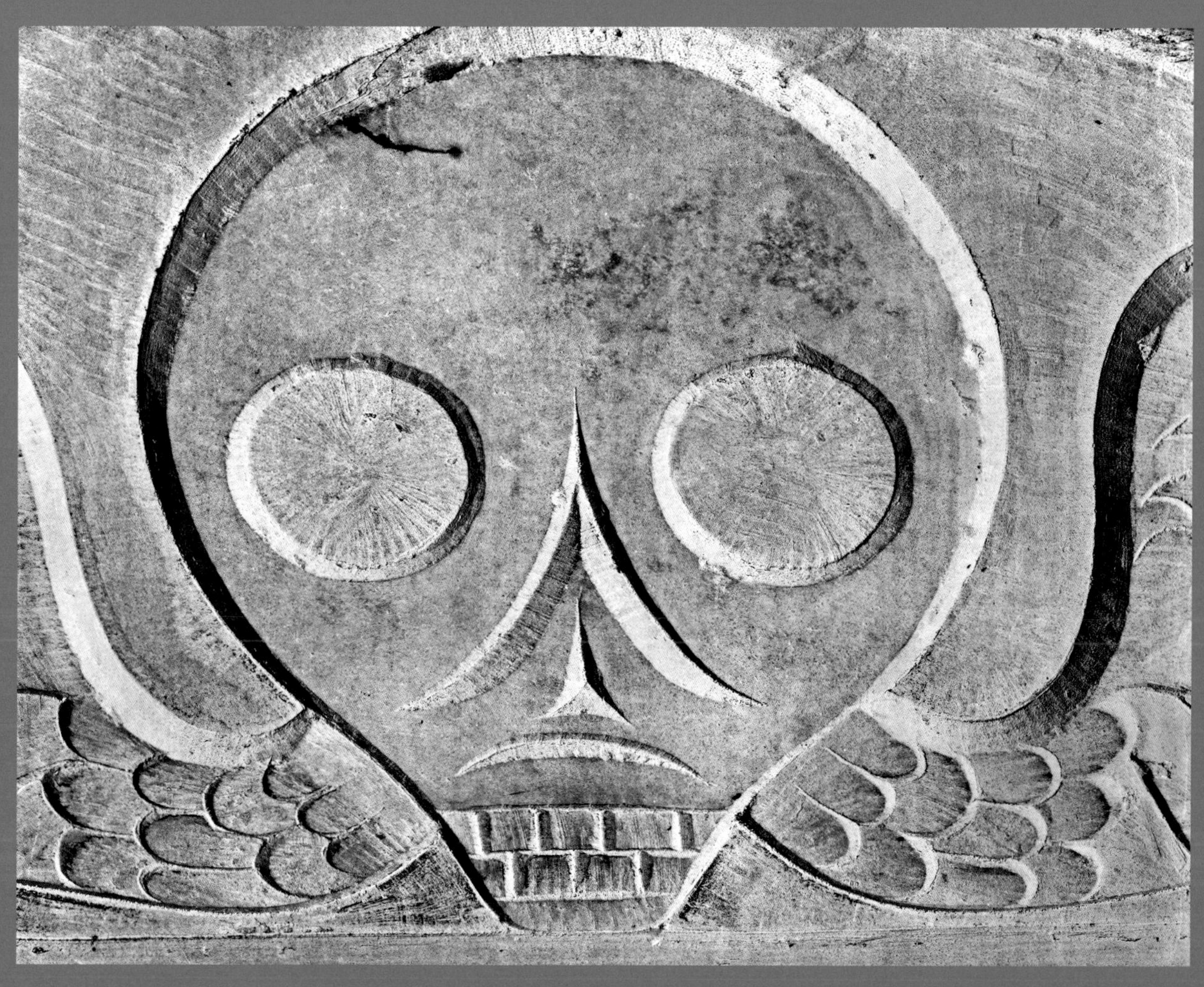

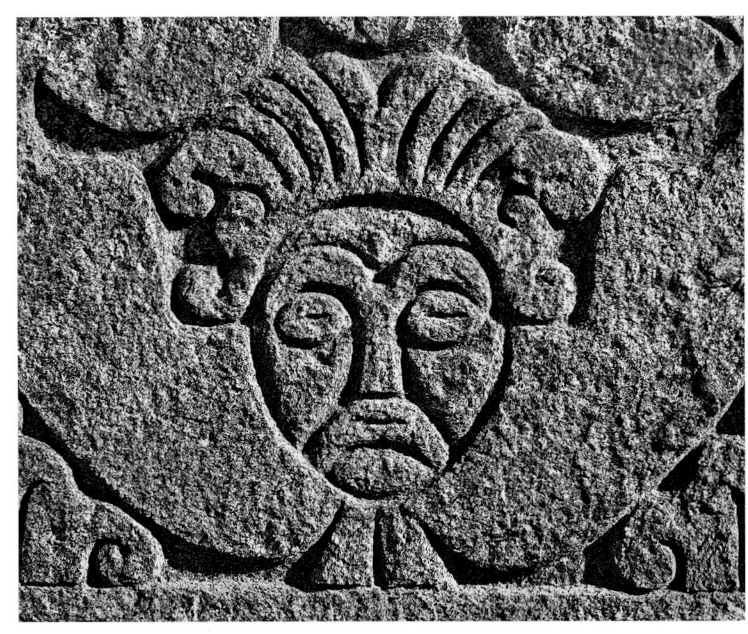

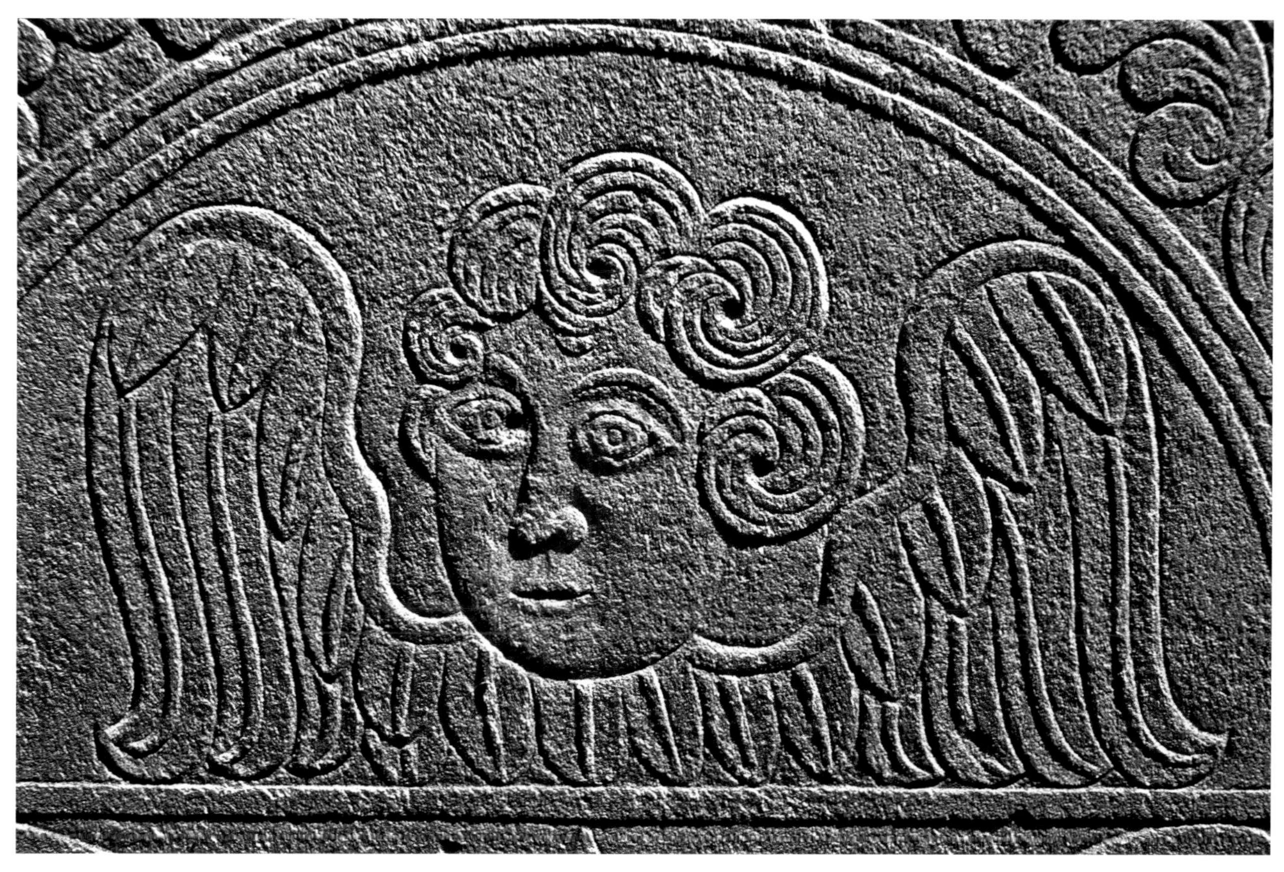

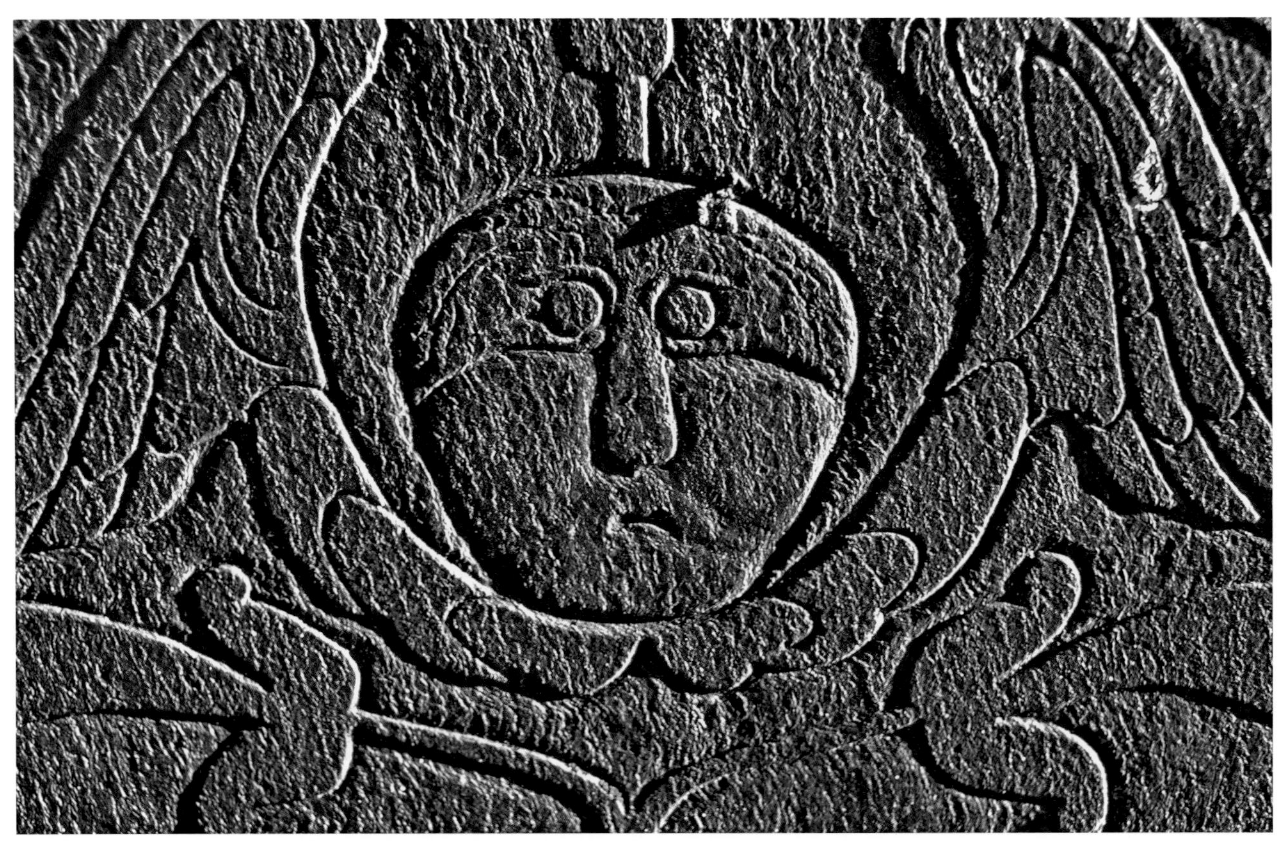

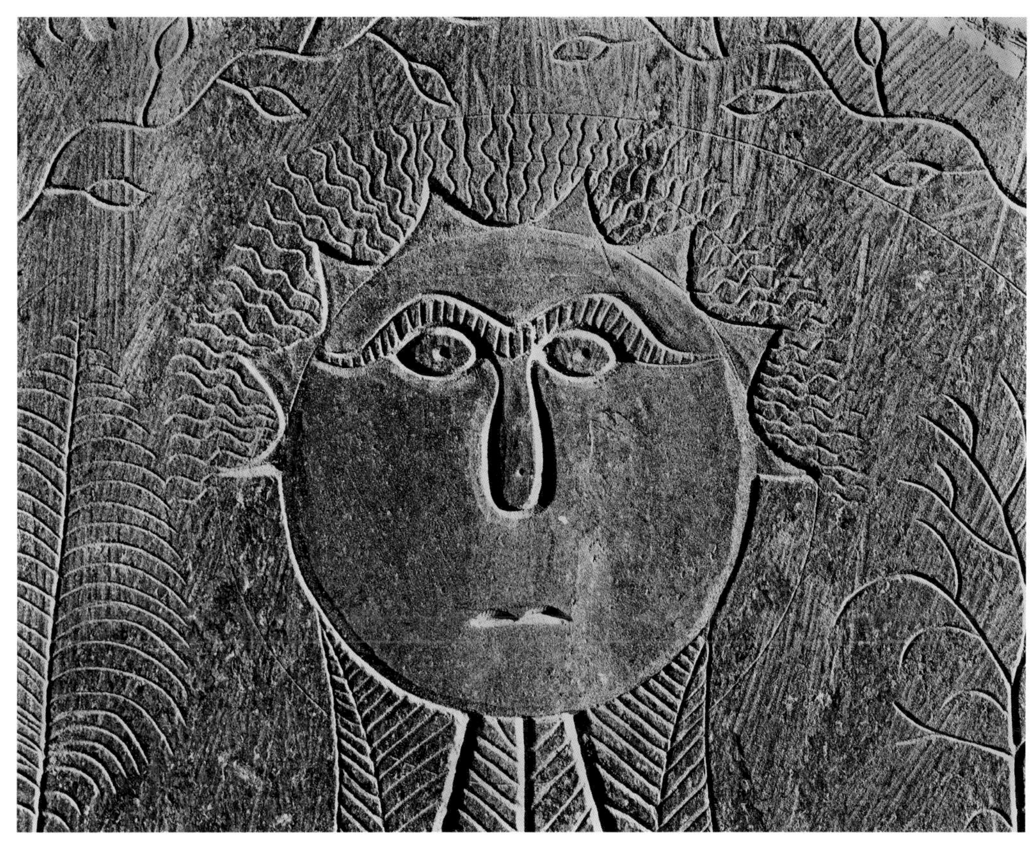

Be it enacted by the Authority of this Court:
that no masters of ships, or seamen, having their vessels riding within any of our harbors shall presume to drink healths, or suffer healths to be drunk within their vessels by day or by night, or to shoot off any gun after the daylight is past or on the Sabbath day, on penalty for every health twenty shillings and for every gun so shot twenty shillings.

"Penalty for Drinking Healths etc. in Ships or Vessels, 1663,"
from the General Laws and Liberties
of the Massachusetts Colony, Cambridge, 1672

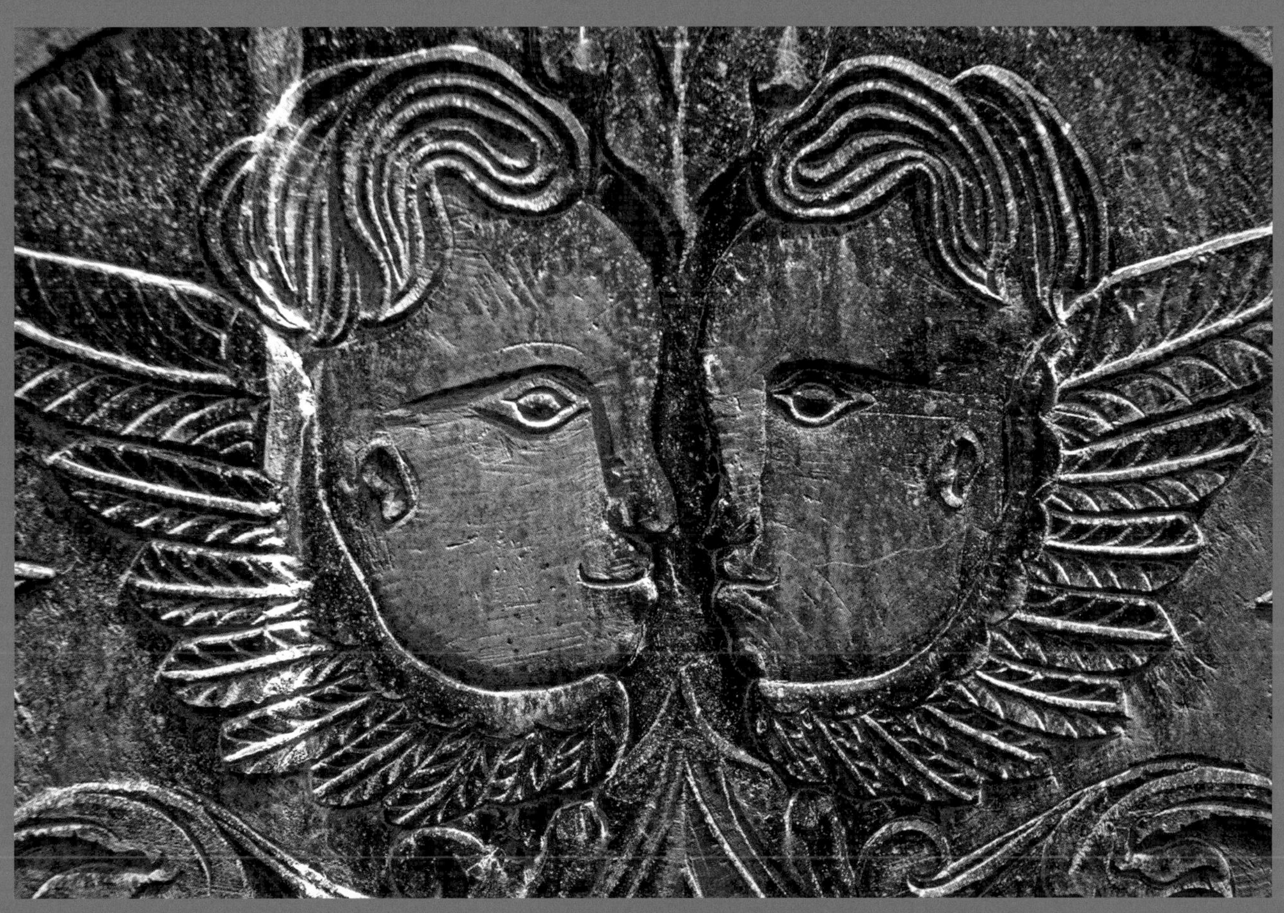

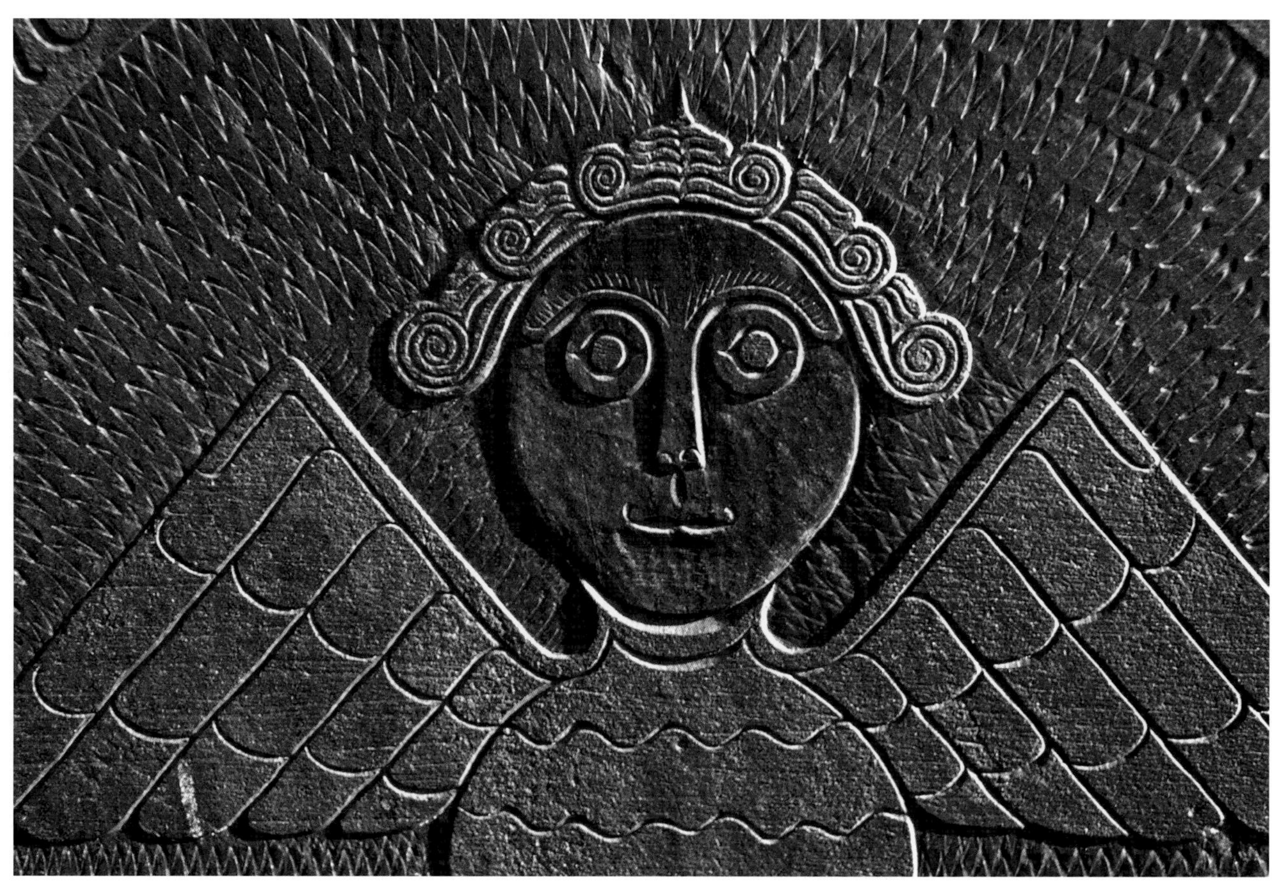

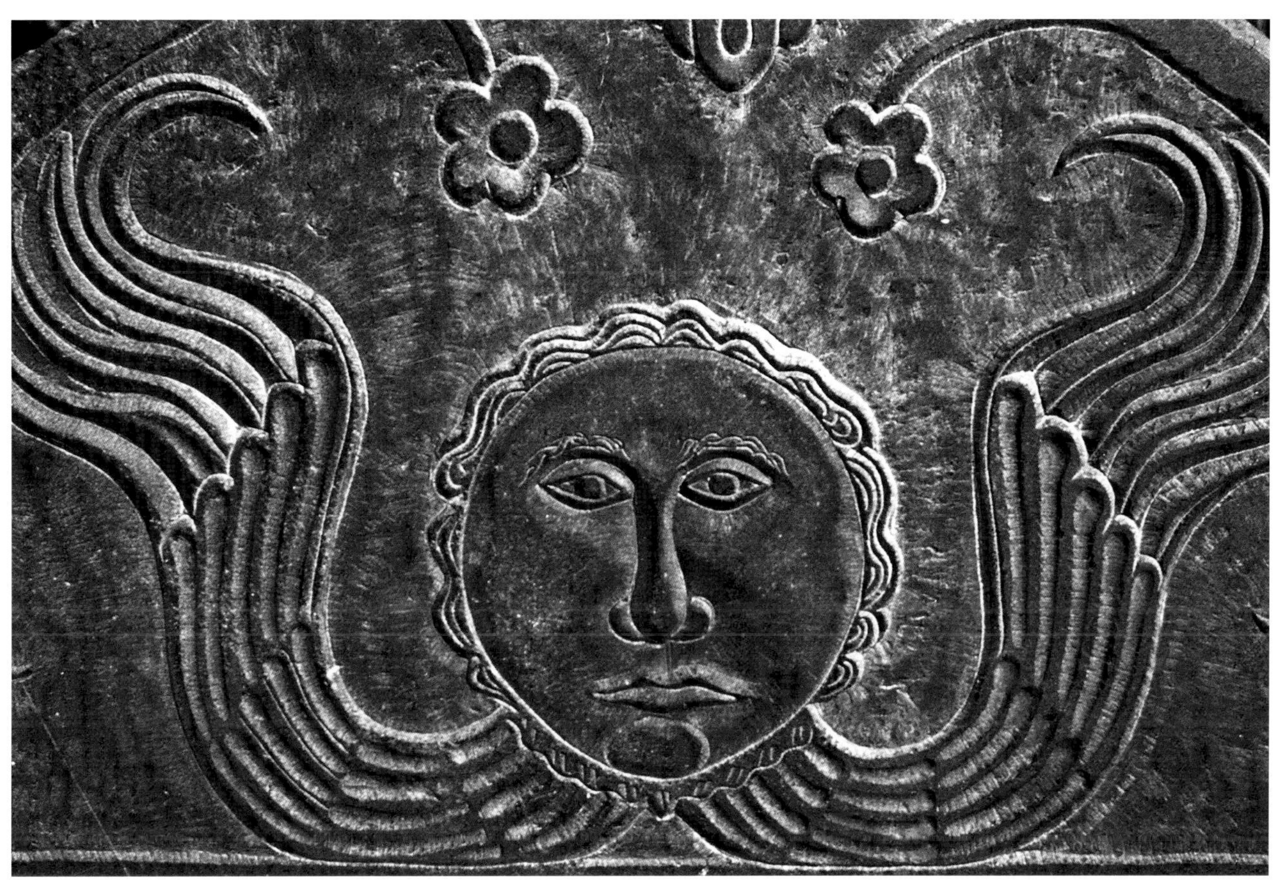

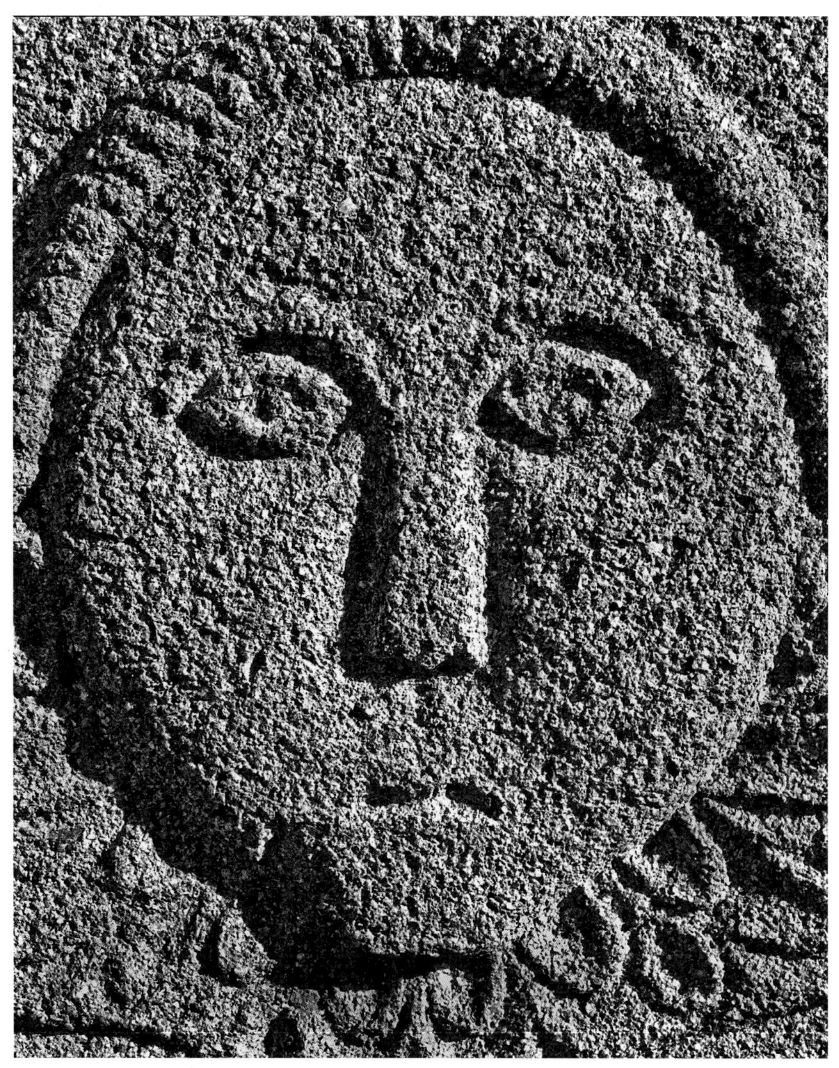

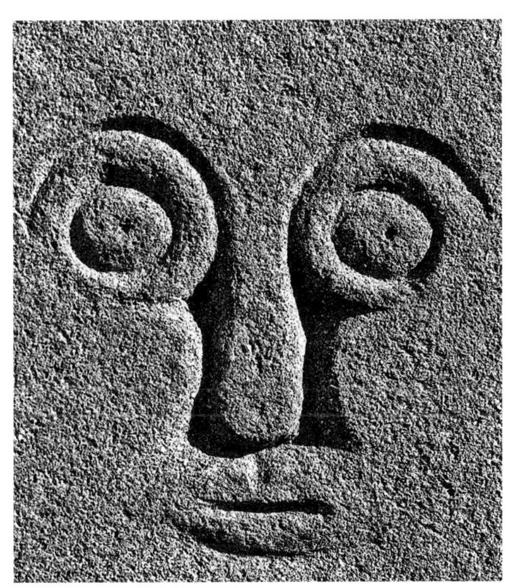

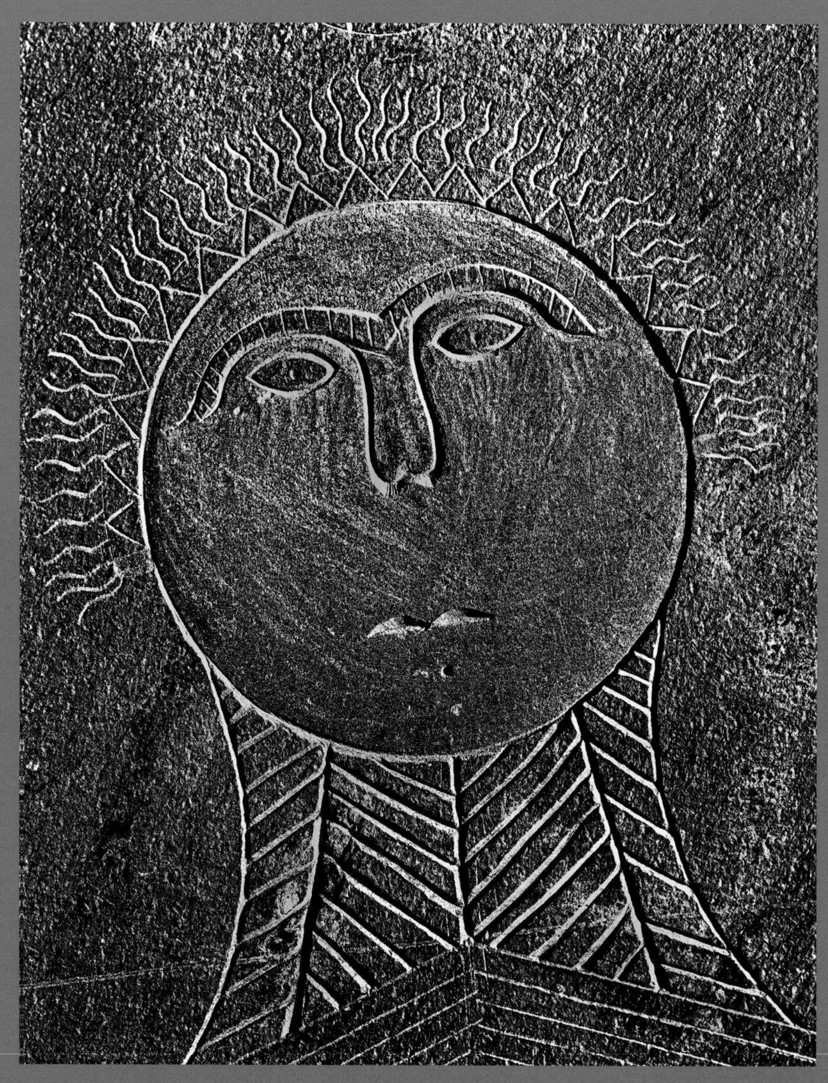

It is not with us as with other men,
whom small things can discourage,
or small discontentments cause to wish
themselves at home againe.

Elder William Brewster

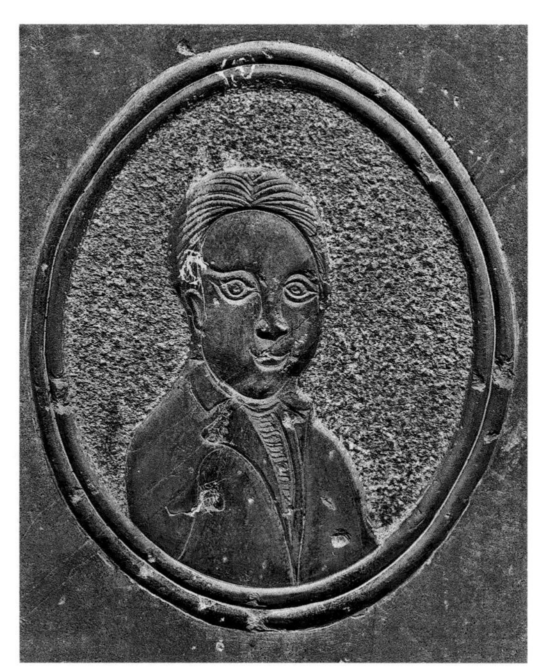

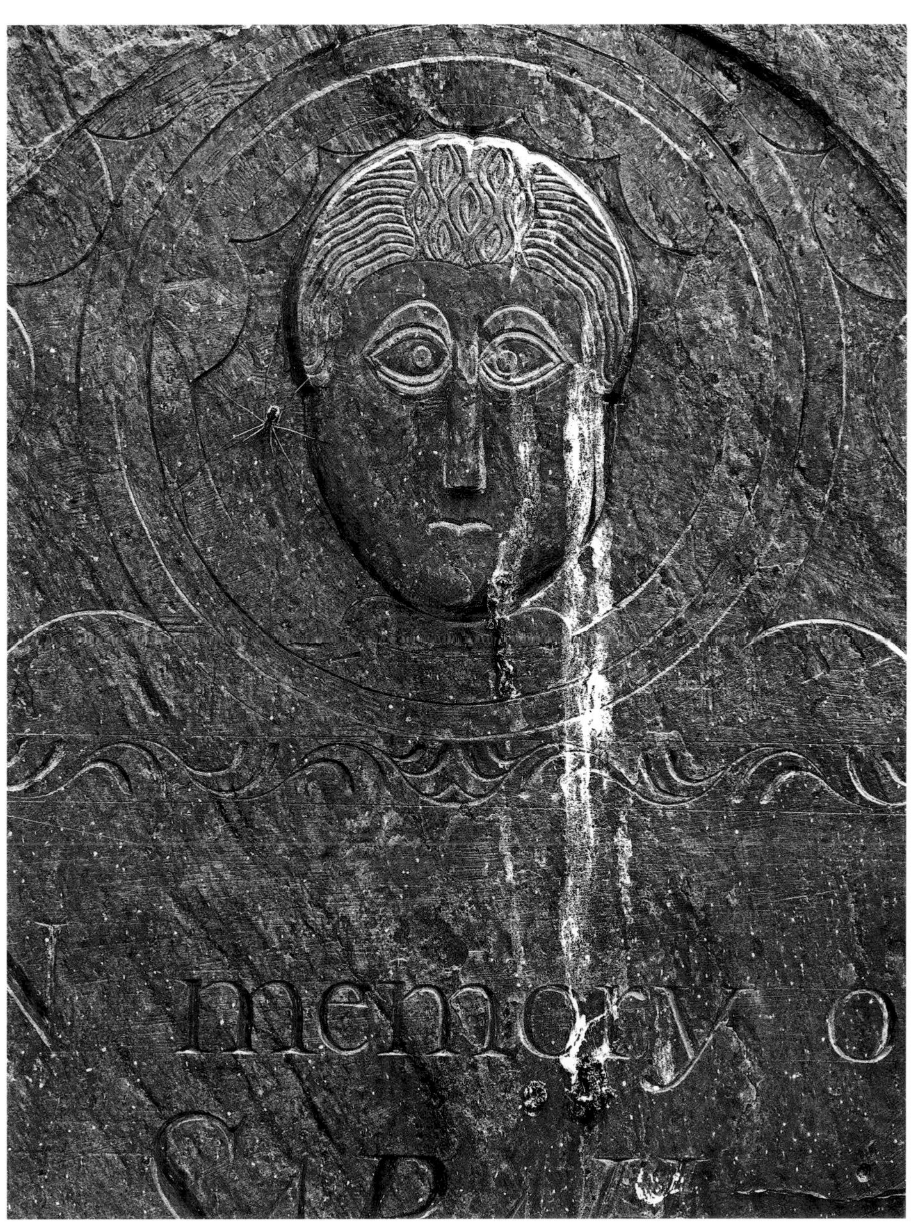
memory

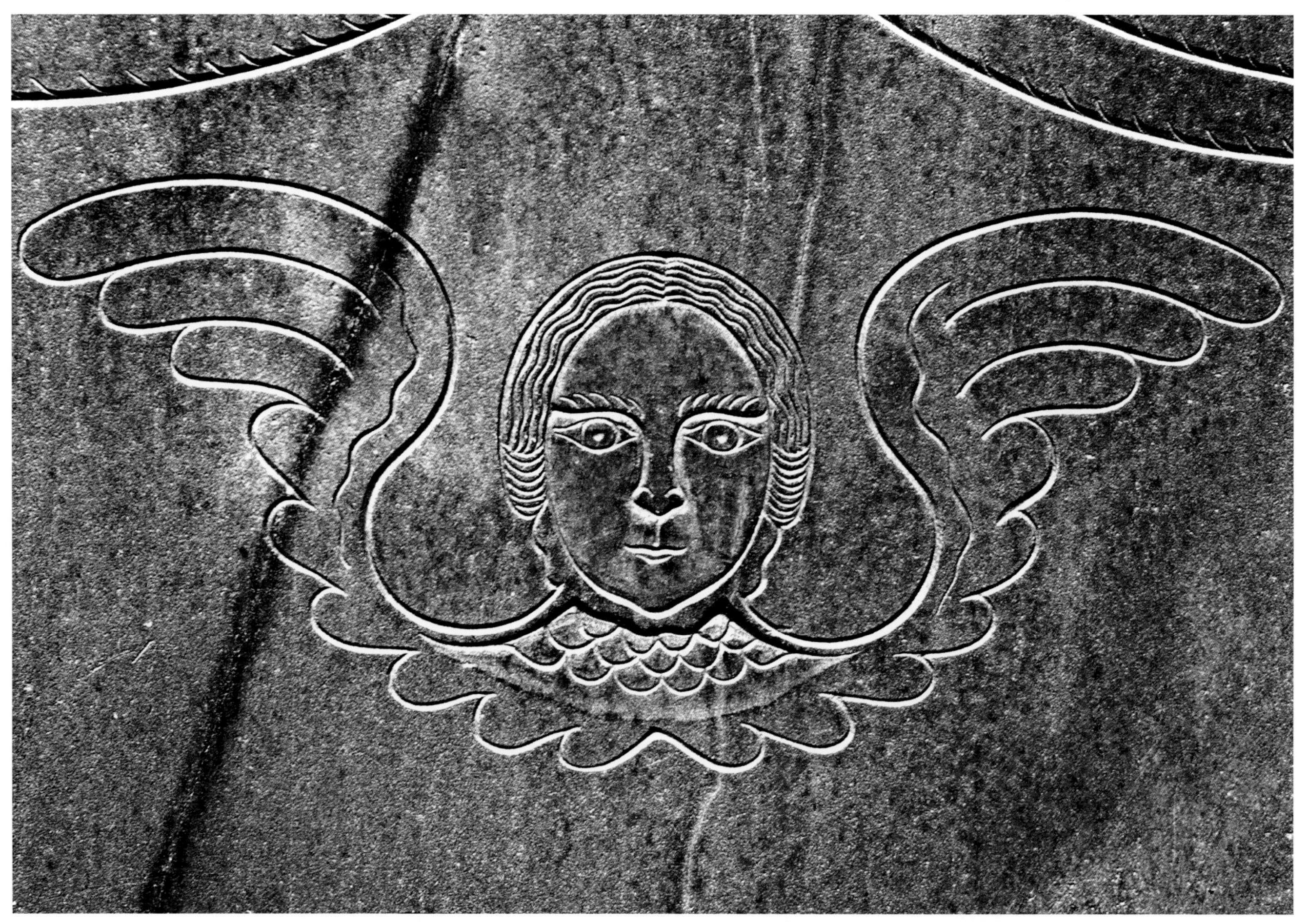

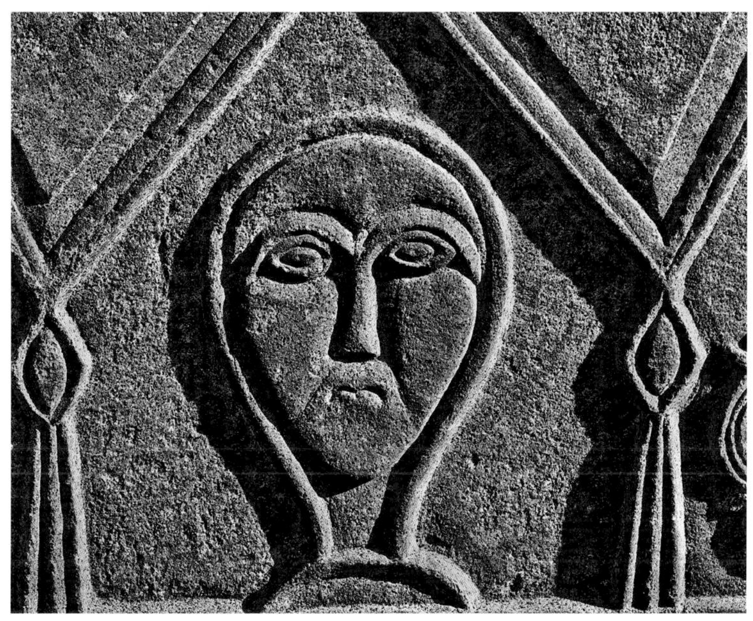

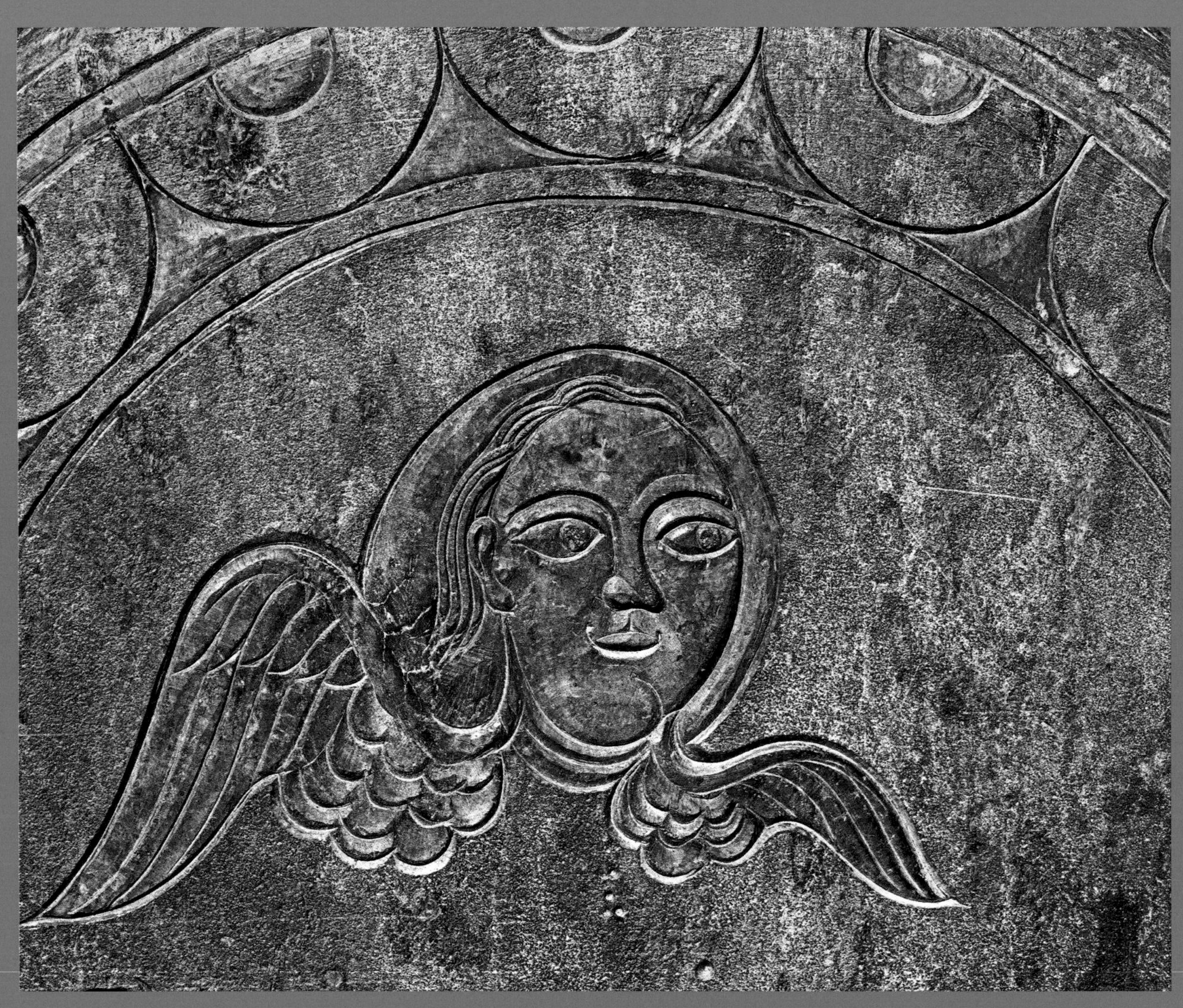

April 11 1712. I saw six swallows together flying and chippering very rapturously.

December 23 1714. Dr. Cotton Mather preaches excellently from Psalms 37, "Trust in the Lord," only spake of the sun being in the center of our system. I think it inconvenient to assert such problems.

Diary of Samuel Sewall

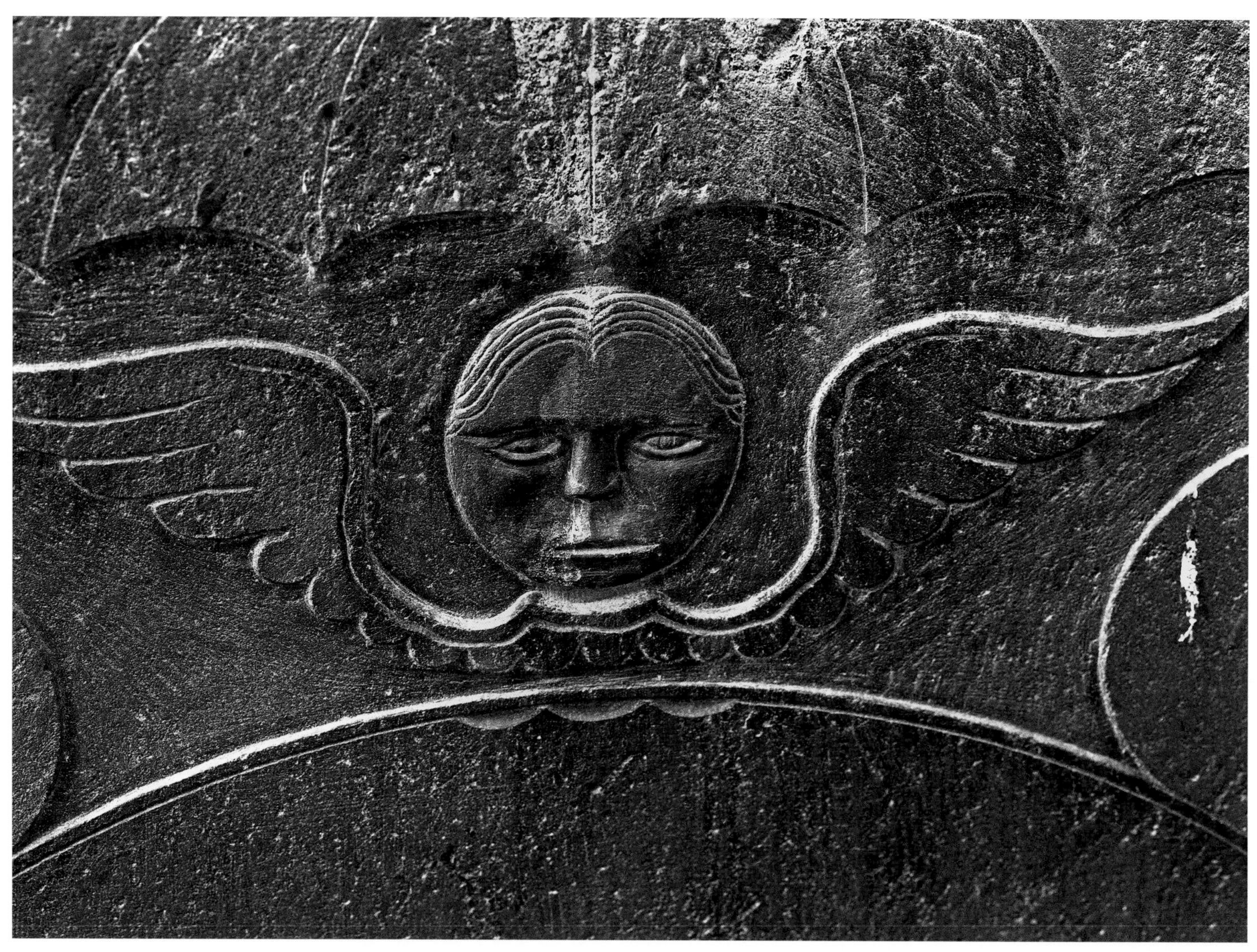

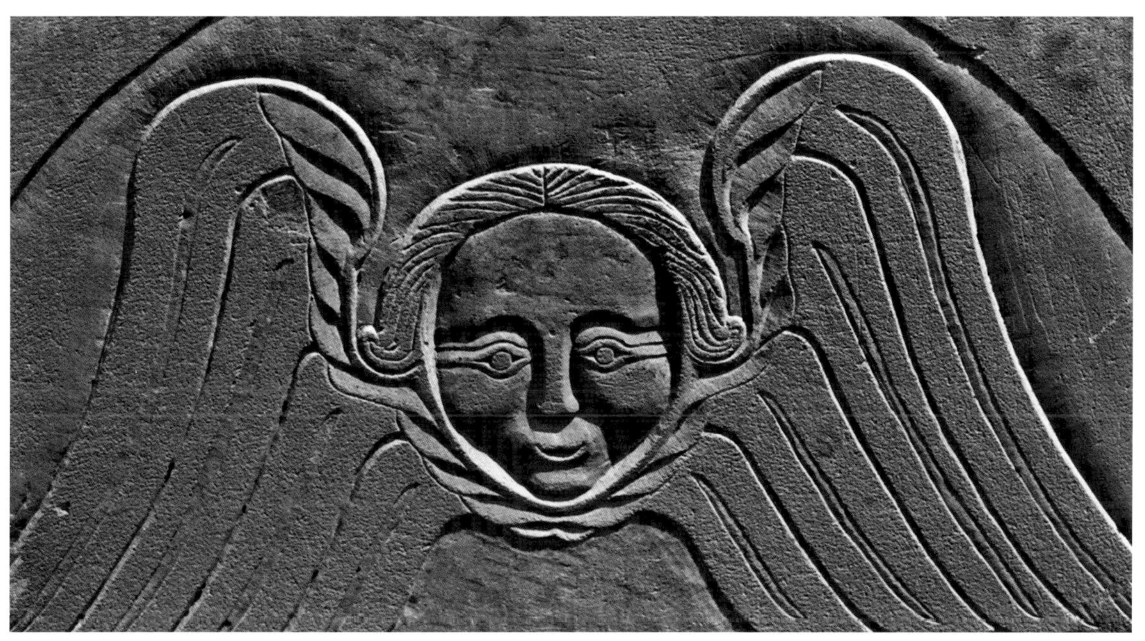

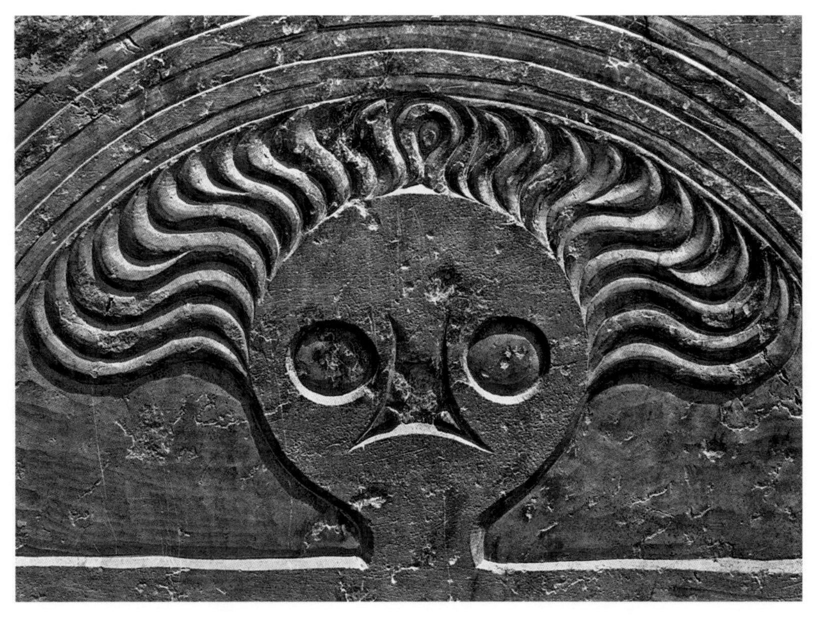

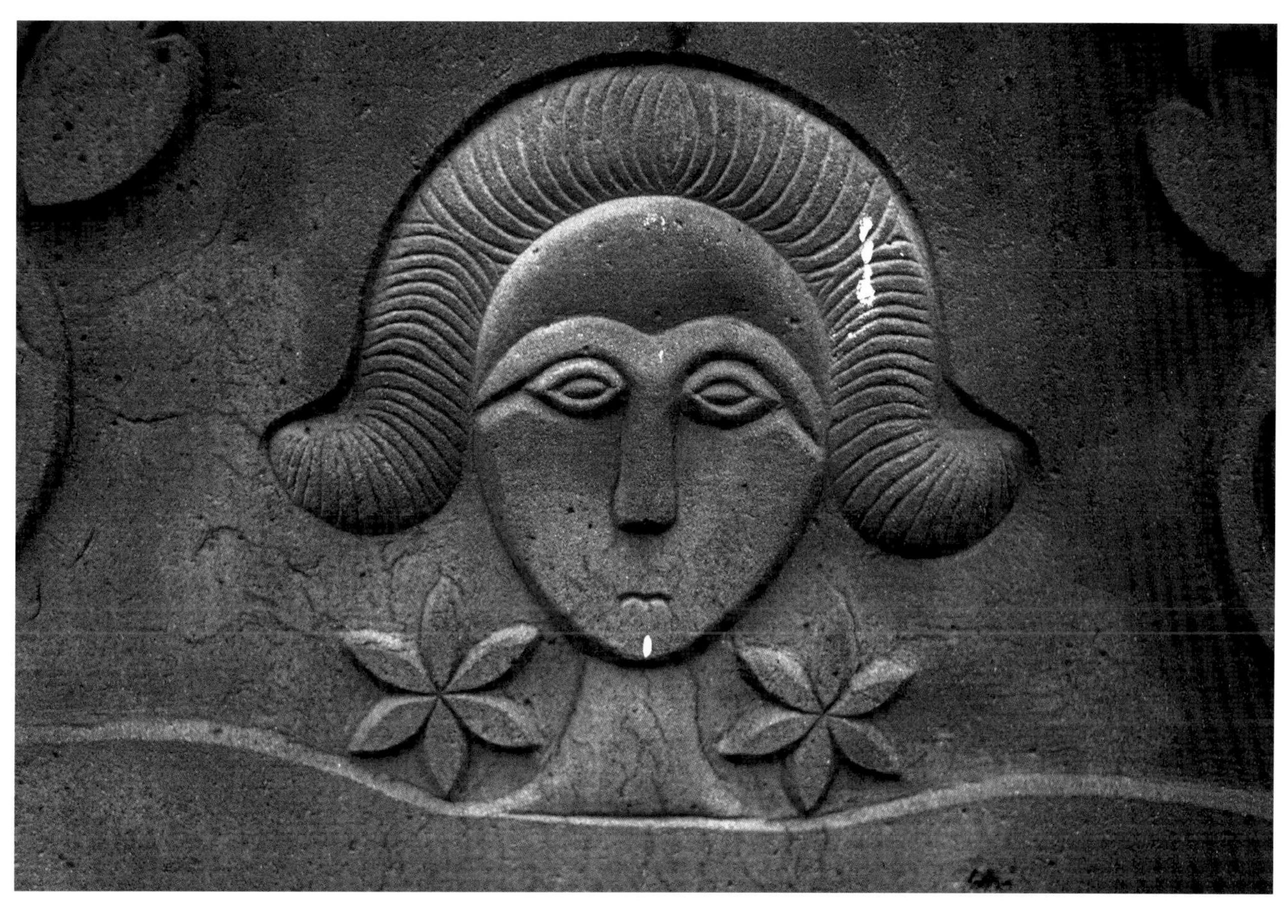

Before his throne a trump is blown,
proclaiming the day of doom,
Forthwith he cries, "Ye dead arise,
and unto judgement come."
No sooner said but 'tis obeyed;
Sepulchers opened are;
Dead bodies all arise at his call,
and's mighty power declare.

"From the Day of Doom,"
by Michael Wigglesworth

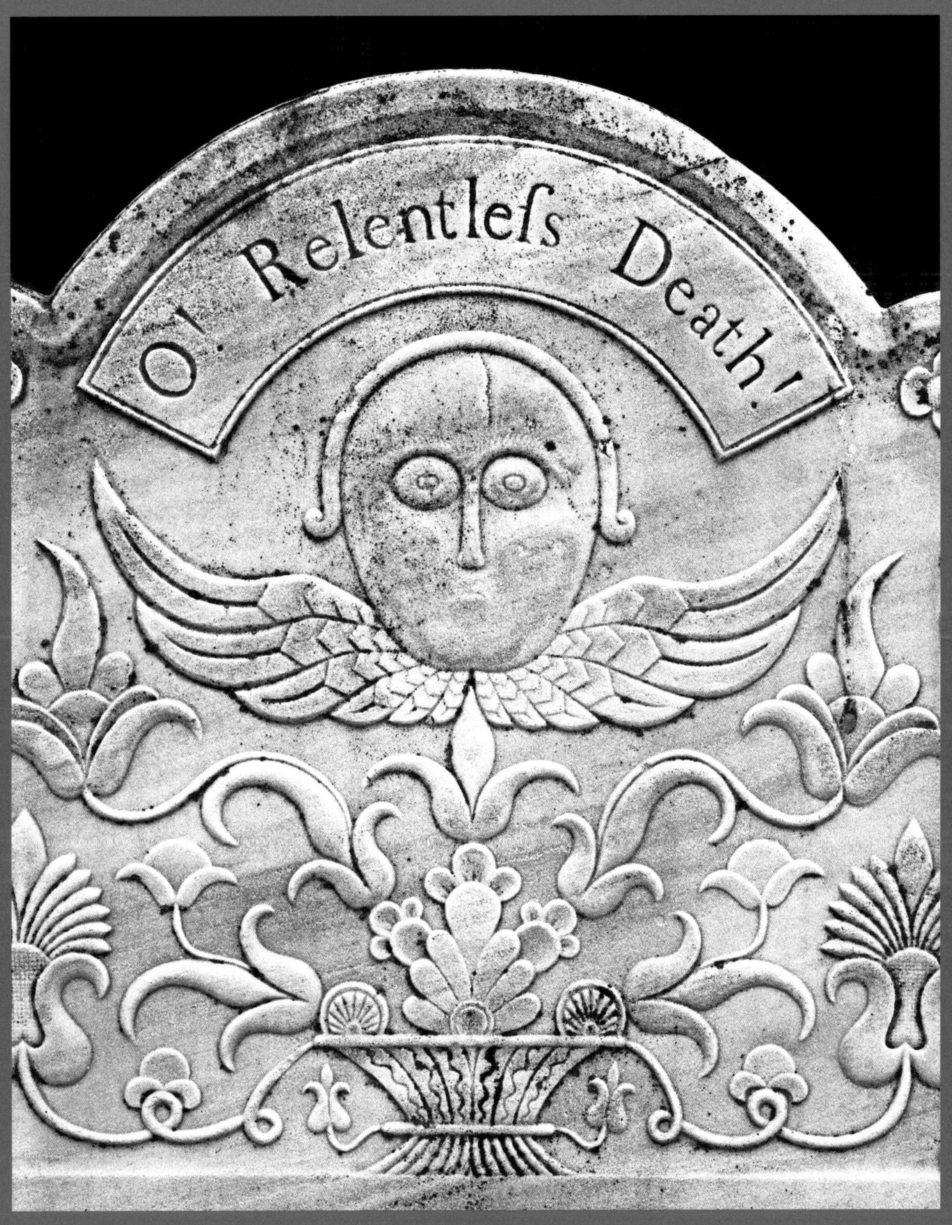
O! Relentless Death!

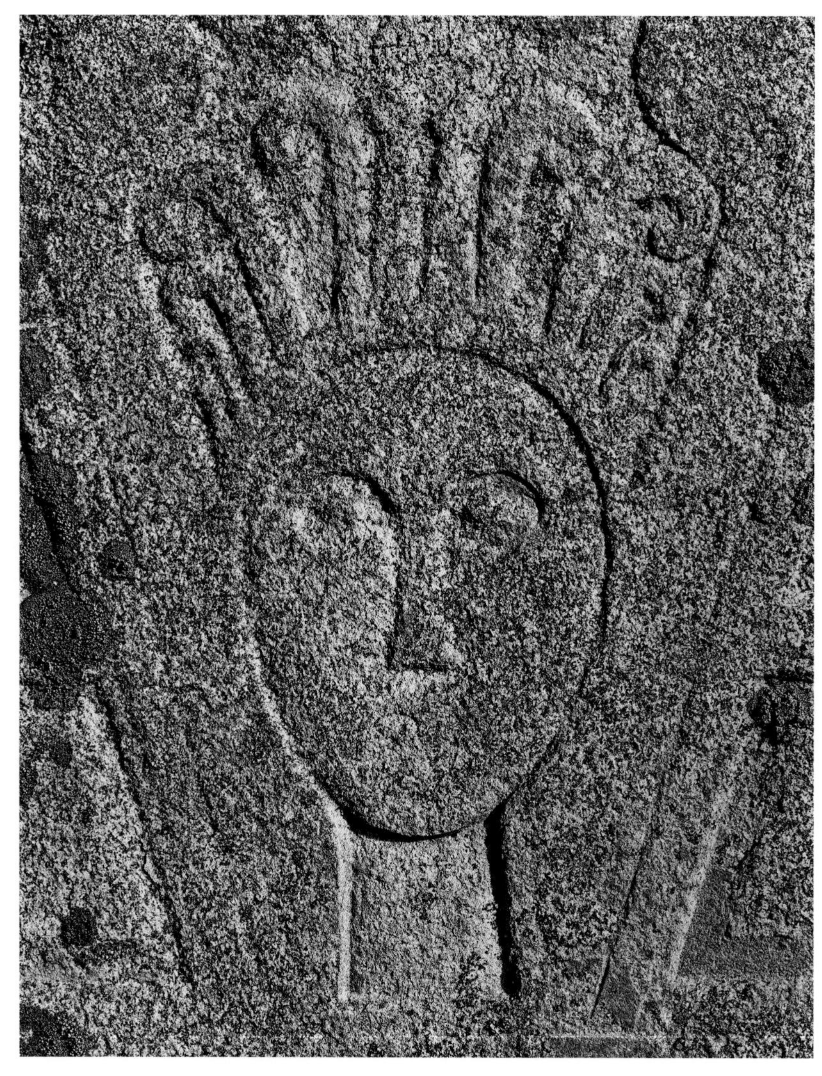

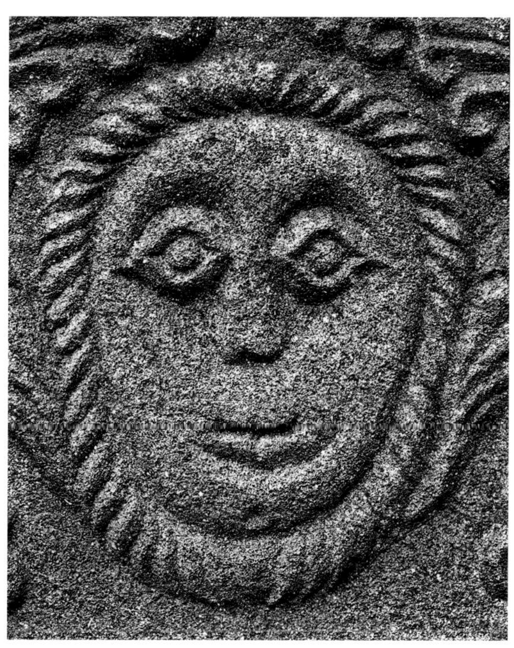

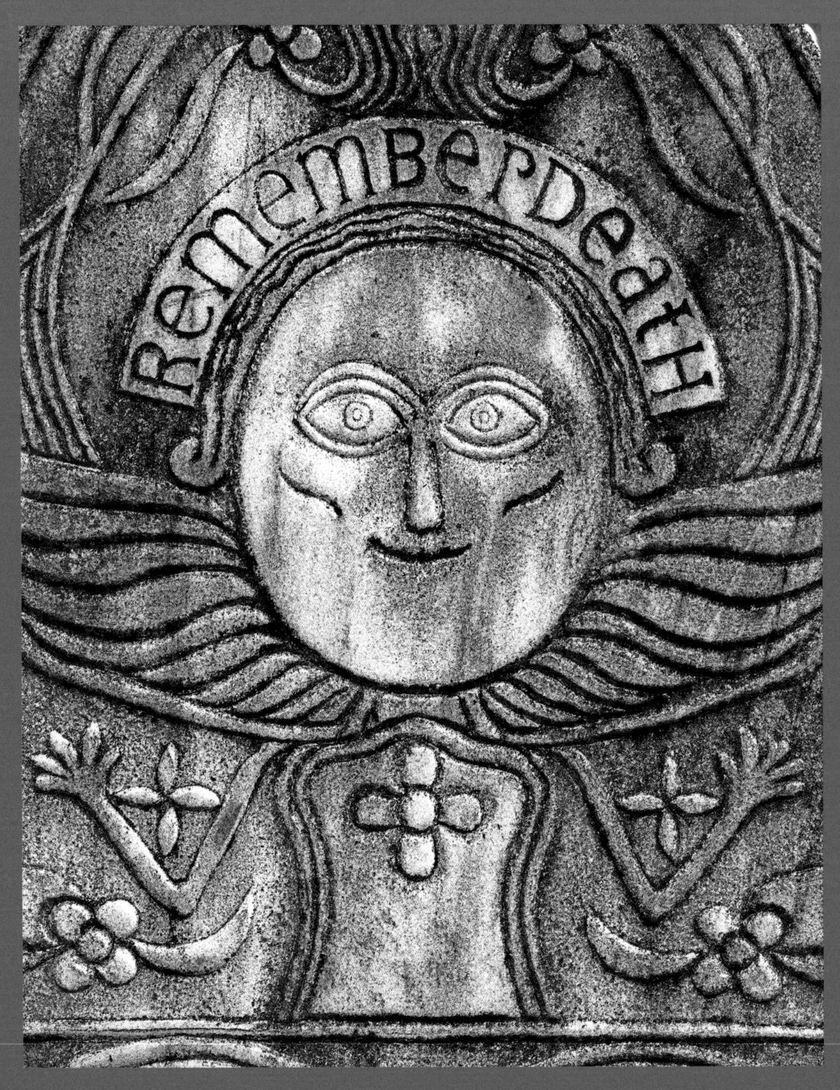
REMEMBER DEATH

The independence and individualism of the Puritan, fostered by the American system of government, were favorable to business enterprise. "Widely conceived" (I quote from Seldes' illuminating chapter "Times of Refreshing") "this was the great American preoccupation. It produced a manufacture suitable to a wide domain. It assumed transportation and the conquest of the wilderness. It involved big business by swift stages. In the half century before the Civil War, the United States was becoming pre-eminently a manufacturing country. By the time Lincoln took office the dominance of industry was obvious. For such a revolution to take place, the minds of the entire population had to be turned unwaveringly to a single object. Call it conquest of the frontier, or progress of mechanics, or desire for gain; when compared with the earlier absorption of the colonists in the affairs of the next world, it amounts to the same thing."

Puritan's Progress (1931), by Arthur Train

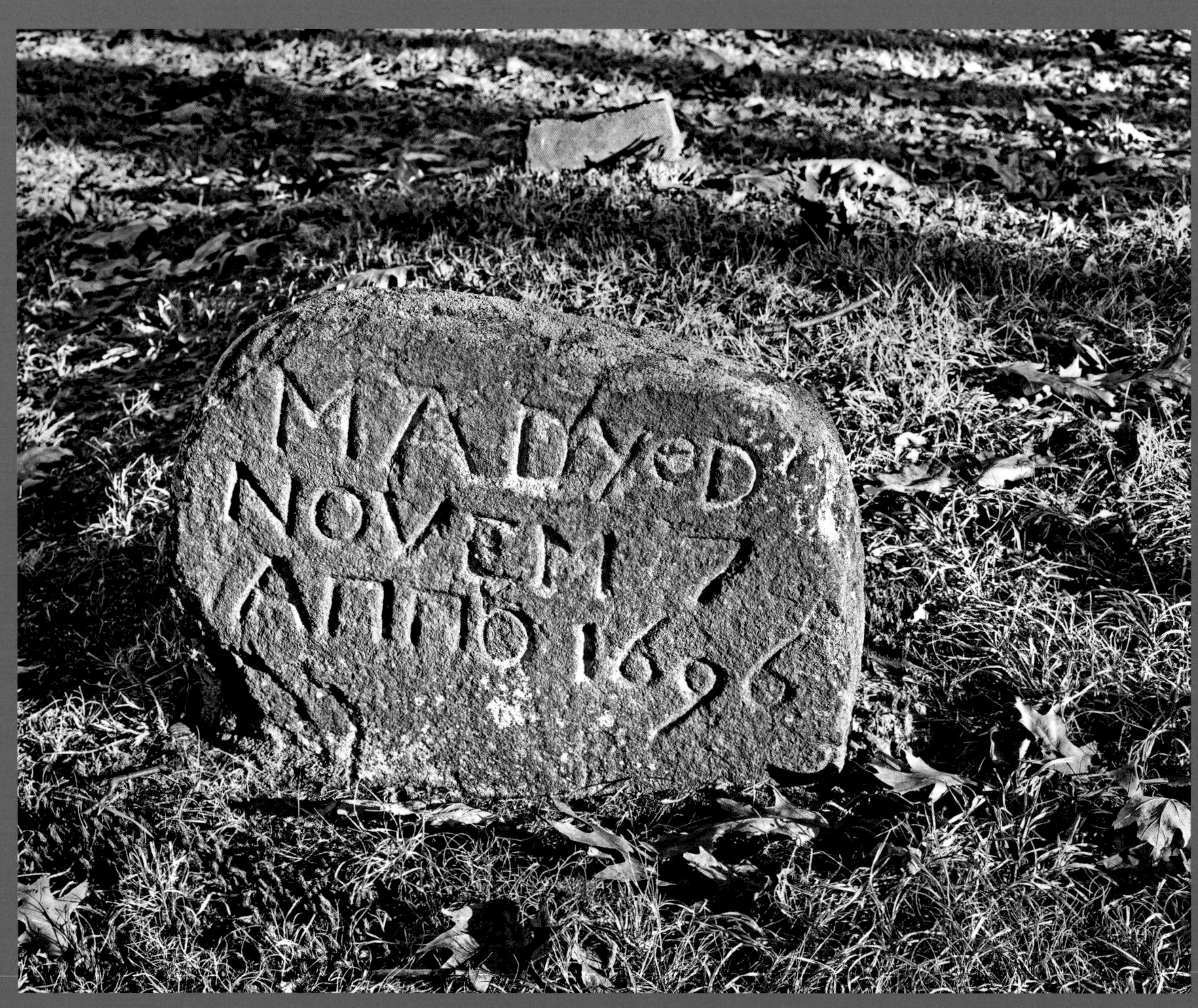
M A DYeD
NOVEM 7
ANNO 1696

PLATES

42 A detail of the John Harwood stone, 1800, Rockingham, Vermont.

43 A detail of the Mary Thoope stone, 1743, Bristol, Rhode Island.

44 A detail of the Mary Brown stone, 1782, Plymouth, Massachusetts.

46 A detail of the Mary Harvey stone, 1785, Deerfield, Massachusetts.

47 A detail of the Martha Green & Infant stone, 1770, Harvard, Massachusetts.

48 A detail of the Mrs. Joanna Pinks stone, 1785, Bernardston, Massachusetts.

49 A detail of the Nathan Gatlin stone, 1793, Deerfield, Massachusetts.

50 A detail of the John Becham stone, 1773, Boston, Massachusetts.

51 A detail of the Samuel Pitman stone, 1757, Newport, Rhode Island.

52 A detail of the Ruth Carter stone, 1797, Boston, Massachusetts.

54 A detail of the John Bartlett stone, 1773, Plymouth, Massachusetts.

55 A detail of the Susanna Jayne stone, 1776, Marblehead, Massachusetts.

56 A detail of the Rufus Kemfield stone, 1787, Belchertown, Massachusetts.

57 A detail of the William Bliss stone, 1782, Belchertown, Massachusetts.

59 A detail of the Ebenezer Wells stone, 1738, Deerfield, Massachusetts.

60 A detail of the Sophia Stoddard stone, 1787, Boston, Massachusetts.

61 A detail of the Hezekiah Root stone, 1792, Belchertown, Massachusetts.

62 A detail of the Capt. Thomas Davis stone, 1785, Plymouth, Massachusetts.

63 A detail of the Mrs. Ann, Wife of Capt. Jonathan Clarke, stone, 1764, Newport, Rhode Island.

64 A detail of the Abigail Wedge stone, 1773, Norwichtown, Connecticut.

66 A detail of the William Warden stone, 1786, Boston, Massachusetts.

67 A detail of the Jemima White stone, 1788, Boston, Massachusetts.

68 A detail of the Melatiah Lothrop stone, 1771, Plymouth, Massachusetts.

69 Unknown, Concord, Massachusetts.

71 A detail of the Elias Olcott stone, 1794, Rockingham, Vermont.

72 A detail of the John Budge stone, 1733, Bristol, Rhode Island.

73 A detail of the Dorothy Carver stone, 1730, Plymouth, Massachusetts.

74 A detail of the Edward Scott stone, 1766, Newport, Rhode Island.

75 A detail of the John Bennet Scott stone, 17??—not readable, Newport, Rhode Island.

77 A detail of the Thomas Barrett stone, 1779, Concord, Massachusetts.

78 A detail of the Rev. William Whitwell stone, 1781, Marblehead, Massachusetts.

79 A detail of the Samuel Dash stone, 1792, Boston, Massachusetts.

80 A detail of the Bethiah Allen stone, 1721, Bristol, Rhode Island.

81 A detail of the Asa White stone, 1781, Rockingham, Vermont.

82 A detail of the Elizabeth Russell stone, 1771, Marblehead, Massachusetts.

84 A detail of the Whiting family stone, 1781, Rockingham, Vermont.

85 A detail of the Edward Seagrave stone, 1797, Grafton, Vermont.

87 A detail of the Sybil Williams stone, 1780, Deerfield, Massachusetts.

88 A detail of the Mrs. Martha Rockwell stone, 1791, South Windsor, Connecticut.

89 A detail of the Ruth Wanton stone, 1773, Newport, Rhode Island.

90 A detail of the Mrs. Silence Gile stone, 1796, Chester, Vermont.

91 A detail of the Margret Campbell stone, 1779, Rockingham, Vermont.

93 A detail of the Nathaniel Band stone, 1773, Boston, Massachusetts.

94 A detail of the Rachel Wolf stone, Rockingham, Vermont.

95 A detail of the Elisabeth Tedder stone, 1769, Marblehead, Massachusetts.

96 A detail of the Mrs. Bathsheba Drake stone, 1795, South Windsor, Connecticut.

97 A detail of the Mrs. Waitstill stone, 1784, South Windsor, Connecticut.

98 A detail of the Samuel Walker stone, 1798, Rockingham, Vermont.

100 A detail of the Capt. John Virgin stone, 1814, Plymouth, Massachusetts.

101 A detail of the Sarah Fox stone, 1783, Bernardston, Massachusetts.

102 A detail of the Mrs. Deli Hudson stone, 1793, Newport, Rhode Island.

103 A detail of the Hannah Dwight stone, 1792, Belchertown, Massachusetts.

104 A detail of the Anna Ferguson stone, 1792, Newport, Rhode Island.

106 A detail of the Abigail Brooks stone, 1795, Concord, Massachusetts.

107 A detail of the Jane Bartlet stone, 1800, Plymouth, Massachusetts.

108 A detail of the Joshua Bramhall stone, 1791, Plymouth, Massachusetts.

109 A detail of the William Stebbins stone, 1797, Longmeadow, Massachusetts.

111 A detail of the Hannah Collins stone, 1797, Dorset, Vermont.

112 Unknown, Belchertown, Massachusetts.

113 A detail of the John Bliss stone, 1780, South Windsor, Connecticut.

114 A detail of the Mary Lyon stone, 1784, Arlington, Vermont.

116 MA DYED ANNO 1696, Deerfield, Massachusetts.

124 A detail of the Mary Brown stone, 1810, Plymouth, Massachusetts.

BIBLIOGRAPHY

Bradford, William, *The History of Plymouth Colony* (Roslyn, NY: Walter J. Black Inc., 1948).

Bunyan, John, *The Pilgrim's Progress* (London: Penguin Books Ltd., 1965).

Burgess, Frederick, *English Churchyard Memorials* (London: Society for Promoting Christian Knowledge, 1979).

Forbes, Harriette Merrifield, *Gravestones of Early New England and the Men Who Made Them, 1653–1800* (Princeton, NJ: Pyne Press, 1973).

Kull, Andrew, *New England Cemeteries: A Collector's Guide* (Brattleboro, VT: Stephen Greene Press, 1975).

Ludwig, Allan, *Graven Images: New England Stonecarving and Its Symbols, 1650–1815* (Middletown, CT: Wesleyan University Press, 1966).

Miller, Perry (Ed.), *The American Puritans: Their Prose and Poetry* (New York: Columbia University Press, 1982).

Miller, Perry, and Thomas H. Johnson (Eds.), *The Puritans: A Sourcebook of Their Writings* (New York: Harper and Row, 1963).

Sewall, Samuel (Ed. M. Halsey Thomas), *The Diary of Samuel Sewall, 1674–1729* (New York: Farrar, Straus and Giroux, 1973).

Stannard, David E., *The Puritan Way of Death: A Study in Religion, Culture and Social Change* (New York: Oxford University Press, 1977).

Tashjian, Dickran and Ann, *Memorials for Children of Change: The Art of Early New England Stonecarving* (Middletown, CT: Wesleyan University Press, 1974).

Taylor, Edward (Ed. Donald E. Stanford), *The Poems of Edward Taylor* (New Haven, CT: Yale University Press, 1960).

Train, Arthur, *Puritan's Progress* (New York: Charles Scribner's Sons, 1931).

ABOUT THE AUTHORS

THOMAS GILSON is the author of *The New England Farm,* a highly praised book of photographs. He worked as managing editor and photographer for the *New England Farmer,* a monthly magazine, and taught black and white photography in Vermont for seventeen years. His photographs have been published and exhibited throughout the United States and England. He lives with his wife in Pine Bush, New York.

WILLIAM GILSON was born and raised in Connecticut and attended the University of Connecticut. His writing has been published in journals and magazines including the *New England Review, Orion,* and *Poetry Salzburg Review.* He lives in Cumbria, England.

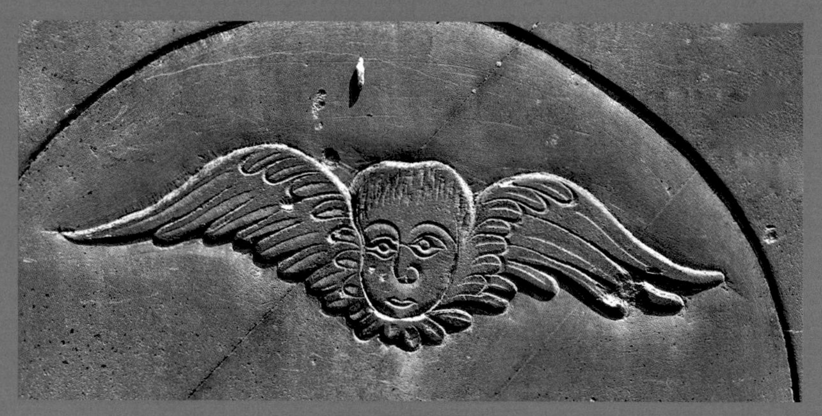